... Poetically Ever After Vol III
Edited by Steve Twelvetree

 Young**Writers**
First published in Great Britain in 2004 by:
Young Writers
Remus House
Coltsfoot Drive
Peterborough
PE2 9JX
Telephone: 01733 890066
Website: www.youngwriters.co.uk

All Rights Reserved

© *Copyright Contributors 2004*

SB ISBN 1 84460 635 X

Foreword

Young Writers was established in 1991 and has been passionately devoted to the promotion of reading and writing in children and young adults ever since. The quest continues today. Young Writers remains as committed to engendering the fostering of burgeoning poetic and literary talent as ever.

This year's Young Writers competition has proven as vibrant and dynamic as ever and we are delighted to present a showcase of the best poetry from across the UK. Each poem has been carefully selected from a wealth of *Once Upon A Rhyme* entries before ultimately being published in this, our twelfth primary school poetry series.

Once again, we have been supremely impressed by the overall high quality of the entries we have received. The imagination, energy and creativity which has gone into each young writer's entry made choosing the best poems a challenging and often difficult but ultimately hugely rewarding task - the general high standard of the work submitted amply vindicating this opportunity to bring their poetry to a larger appreciative audience.

We sincerely hope you are pleased with our final selection and that you will enjoy *Once Upon A Rhyme . . . Poetically Ever After Vol III* for many years to come.

Contents

Alex Cook (7)	1
Ryan Cammack (10)	1
Rory Kelham (9)	2
Chantelle Ampomah (11)	2
Aisha Iqbal (12)	3
Stephanie Martin (11)	4
Rebecca Richards (9)	4
Roddy Macrae (11)	5
Nathan Heels (10)	5
Olivia Ireson (11)	6
Ilan Strul (11)	6
Aaron Kelly (7)	6

Aberdour School, Tadworth

Harriet Walsh (10)	7
Ben Smith (9)	7
Camilla Shopland (10)	8
Sam Boulton (9)	8
Jessica Scholfield (9)	9
Jack Cotsworth (8)	9
Daniel Coppen (10)	10
Jacob Ansell (11)	10
Ben Wackett (9)	11
Alex Wade (10)	11
Hannah Pipe (10)	12
Sophia Syed (9)	12
Emma Ward (10)	13
Thomas Hornsey (10)	14
Thomas Bradbury (8)	14
Adam Creswell (8)	15
Laura Sharman (11)	15
Harry Ellison (8)	16
Megan Brockman (9)	16
Oliver Reavley (9)	17
Joshua Morris (9)	17
Ollie Batchelor (10)	18
Christopher Gee (10)	18
Antony Kalindjian (11)	19
Eiméar Monaghan (9)	19

Matthew Van-Noort-Pendleton (8)	20
Gregory Hodgson (8)	20
Alex Huber (11)	21
Oliver Robinson (11)	21
Rebecca Mullett (9)	22
James Barlow (9)	22
Jessica Kay-Ogunsola (11)	23
Naohiro Hattori (10)	24
Ben Aldersley (11)	25
James Saunders (9)	25
Kiran Govekar (11)	26
Zoe Rutherford (11)	26
Harry Carpenter (10)	27
Sam Adams (8)	27
Jamie Beard (10)	28
Natasha Moore (11)	28
Calum Watt (10)	29
Guy Lester (9)	30
Connie Woollen (10)	30
James Pine (9)	31
Callum White (11)	31
Sophie Ayles (8)	32
Daniel Godden (11)	32
Alisdair Kemp (11)	33
Matthew Ayles (11)	33
Samuel Lee (11)	34
Thomas Eades (8)	34
Richard Hawkins (11)	35

Ashdon CP School, Saffron Walden
Sebastian Patrick (6)	35

Crathes Primary School, Banchory
Amy Longmore (10)	35

Dalry Primary School, Edinburgh
Darren McLuskie (10)	36
David Glass (11)	36
Kandice Wood (10)	37
Farhan Ali (10)	37

Ferguslie Primary School, Paisley
  Natanya Feeley (10) — 38
  Jamie Skalley (10) — 38
  Jordan Foster (9) — 38
  Lauren McPhee (9) — 39
  Nicola Moran (9) — 39
  Lisa Humphries (9) — 39

Knaphill Junior School, Woking
  Matthew Furniss (11) — 40
  Ben Howes (11) — 41
  Priyanka Modgill (11) — 41
  Ellie Bostock (11) — 42
  Chelsea Norman (11) — 42
  Billy Lee (10) — 43
  Charlie Simms (11) — 43
  Riandra Moynihan (11) — 44
  Lucy Franklin (11) — 44
  Shaunii Robb (11) — 45
  Hannah Deluce (11) — 45
  Peter Prince (11) — 45
  Alex Paterson (11) — 46
  Chris Warburn (11) — 46
  Katie Winter (11) — 46
  Laura Cugulliere (11) — 47
  Kerry Dwan (10) — 47
  Sam Smith (11) — 47
  Emma Crampton (11) — 48
  Emma England (11) — 48
  Oliver Benstead (11) — 49
  Charlotte Masson (11) — 49
  Steven Pattenden (11) — 50
  Leah Partridge (10) — 50
  Emily Laybourn (11) — 51
  Taylor Shephard (11) — 51
  Daniella White (11) — 52
  Allana King (11) — 53
  Amybeth Edwards (11) — 53
  Elizabeth Biggs (11) — 53
  Jess Warwick (11) — 54
  Bradley Bayliss (11) — 54

Naomi Gale (11)	55
Jen Levy (10)	55
Simon Gregory (11)	56
Emma Spencer (11)	56
Louise Cobban (11)	57

Knowepark Primary School, Selkirk

Jack Duncan (8)	57

Lack Primary School, Enniskillen

Rachael Keys (9)	58
Kylie Noble (10)	58
Lorna Graham (10)	59
Zana Bratton (9)	59
Emma Forbes (10)	60
Robert Corry (11)	60
Alison Neville (10)	61
Emma Beacom (11)	61
Jemma Walker (10)	62
Julie Weir (9)	62
Gail Woods (10)	63
Nathanael Brown (11)	64

Leighfield Primary School, Uppingham

Abigail Thompson-O'Connor	65
Charlotte Gregg (7)	65
Edgar Ellis (8)	65
Molly Feely (9)	66
Grace Gutteridge (9)	66
Henry Jones (9)	67
Robert Fox (9)	67
George Scott (9)	67
Luke Roberts (11)	68
Hannah Rose (8)	68
Benjamin Kind & Joshua Wedge (11)	69
Ryan Bennett (10)	69
Elizabeth Wignall (11)	70
Catherine Crook (9)	70
Georgia Huzar (11)	71
Phoebe Toms (9)	71

Georgina Mattock (11)	72
Charlie Pallett (9)	72
Laura Buzzard (11)	73
Olivia Cowood (9)	73
William Raynes (11)	74
Edward Wignall (9)	74
Adam Willars (11)	75
Samuel Allen (10)	75
Jessica Gray (11)	76
Laura Williams (11)	76
Laura Wilks (10)	77
Kathryn Robinson (11)	77
Ruth Corbet (11)	78
Hannah Gregg (9)	78
Jessica Torbell (11)	79
Elliot Todd (11)	79
Bethany Prior (10)	80
Grace Hudson (10)	80
Victoria Neill (11)	81
Hannah Ellwood (9)	81
Grace Sanders (11)	82
Claire Garley (10)	82
Bradley Toms (11)	83
Louise Garley (10)	83
Holly Montagnon (11)	84
Sian Evans (10)	84
Samuel Evans (11)	85
Jack De Wet (6)	85
Isaac Parr (11)	86
Douglas J Douglas (6)	86
Tilly Jones (11)	87
Francis Wignall (5)	87
Rachelle Bartlett (11)	88
Rebecca Wootton (5)	88
Hector Thorne (6)	89
James Flavell (6)	89
Adam Roberts (6)	89
Tessa Cooper (7)	90
Oliver Dean (5)	91
Robert Johnson (7)	91
Jack Morris (6)	91
Melissa Willars (5)	91

Amy Hunting (7)	92
Harry Hathaway (7)	92
William Johnson (7)	92
Lewis Jennings (7)	93
Beatrix Wignall (7)	93
Megan Wright (7)	93
Calypso Keightley (7)	94
Emogene Bromwich (7)	94
Hollie Denney (7)	94

Moorland Primary School, Cardiff

Leighton Davies (11)	95

Mundford Primary School, Thetford

Charlotte Hogg (8)	95
Hannah Dolman (9)	96
Christopher Walkey (9)	96
Sophie Boulton (8)	97
Megan Wharf (8)	97
James Elwood (8)	98
Halima Khan (8)	98
Ashlie White (8)	99
Daniel Nicholls (10)	99
Darryl Wilson (10)	100
Leona Stubbings (8)	100
Carl Brooks (10)	101
Tony Way (10)	101
Jake Patrick (10)	101
Fern Stannett (9)	102

Old Warren Primary School, Lisburn

Rebecca Brown (9)	102
Kayleigh Laybourn-Houston (10)	103
Neal Archer (7)	103
Kirsty Gorman	104
Samuel Dowds (8)	104
Glenn McCutcheon (8)	105

Poringland Primary School, Poringland
Adam Collins (7) — 105
Gareth Phipps (8) — 105
William Warnes (7) — 105

Premnay School, Insch
Zoe Curtis (11) — 106
Emma Sim (9) — 106

St Eugene's Primary School, Knocks
Rachael Feely (8) — 107
Sarah McGoldrick (9) — 107
Lisa Ingram (9) — 108
Ryan Carney (7) — 108
Colin Logan (9) — 109
Aoife Maguire (8) — 109
Eimir Maguire (8) — 110
Mark O'Reilly (9) — 110
Raymond Logan (10) — 111
Cathal O'Neill (9) — 111
Sinead Rice (10) — 112

St Joseph's Catholic Primary School, Wesham
Joely Emms (9) — 112
Thomas Thain (7) — 113
Laura Hall (8) — 113
Bradley Johnson (9) — 114
Joseph Clarke (8) — 115

St Stephen's CE Junior School, Twickenham
Olivia Wylde (10) — 115
Molly Riglin (9) — 116
Ben Winward (7) — 116
Lottie Fogg (7) — 117
Billy Cohen (8) — 117
Caitlin Blyth (8) — 117
Alexandria Gutman (7) — 118
Hebe Naylor (7) — 118
William Jenkins (7) — 118
Lucy Theobald (8) — 119

Matthew Parsons (7)	119
Madeline Ralph (7)	119
Carys Thomson (7)	120
Megan Jones (7)	120
Phoebe Tupper (7)	121
Kaja Redler (7)	121
Lucy Whitear (8)	121
Emma Davies (8)	122
Thomas Drew (7)	122
Matthew Fletcher (8)	122
Henry Day (8)	123
Ruby Woolfe (9)	123
Eleanor McKone (7)	124

Senacre Wood Primary School, Maidstone

Ben Houghton (10)	124
Alice Manser (11)	125
Michael Mannell (11)	125
Kirsty Foster (11)	126
Anthony Luck (11)	127
Samantha Craig (10)	127
Lewis Nicholson (11)	128
Natasha Tucker (11)	129
Craig Tupper (11)	130
Jac Tompsett (11)	130
Jay Kitchenham (10)	131
Lee Tucker (11)	131
Jake Brown (11)	132
Zoe Woodcock (11)	133
Jason Goodwin (11)	134
Emily Gilham (10)	135
James Manners (11)	136
Chloe Penfold (10)	137

Southwood Primary School, Dagenham

Mark Ferrari (10)	137
Sara Smith (10)	138
Mollie Sheridan (10)	138
Melisa Mert (10)	138
Kurt Chilvers (10)	139
Amy Ebbs (10)	139

Adam Wiffen (9)	139
Taylor Paradise (10)	140
James Boxall (10)	140
Francesca Duffin (10)	140
Charlie Pennington (8)	141
Kathryn Smith (8)	141
Gus Hawkes (8)	141
Roma Alcknaviciute	142
Lauren Docherty (10)	142
Katie Simpson (9)	143
Anna Smith (9)	143
Jerry Lewis (8)	144
Frank Griffin	144
Emileigh Day (9)	145
Sophie Arthur (10)	145
Danni Redgrave (11)	146
Abigail O'Shea (8)	146
Ross Worthing (11)	147
Ryan Bell (8)	147
Kerry Davies (11)	148
Rachel Ellis (10)	148
Jay Wheeler (9)	149
Kate Wallace (8)	149
Sarah Jones (10)	150
Georgie Read (8)	150
Gemma Smith (11)	151
Kathryne Hamilton (10)	151
Megan Little (9)	152
James Flexen-Tin (9)	152
Lewis Keble (10)	153
Emily Richardson (10)	153
Luke Van Gelder (9)	154
Edward Searle (11)	154
Muhamet Halilaj (10)	154
Mitchell Oxborrow (8)	155
Christopher Cooper (11)	155
Matthew Hamilton (8)	156
Lewis Stevens (7)	156
Beth Willcocks (10)	157
Jordan Mabey (8)	157
David Crampton (11)	158
Kirsty Simpson (8)	158

Michael Howes (11)	159
Abigail Davies (8)	159
Paige Berrecloth (9)	160
Jennifer Smith (8)	160
Ellie Terry (9)	161
Arif Hossain (11)	161
Luke Bartolo (11)	161
Hammad Khan (7)	162
Ben Skinner (8)	162
John Cooper (8)	162
Millennia Severino (8)	163
Liam Peters (8)	163
Zaid Jilani (8)	164
Alfie Yeaman (8)	164
Sam Berrecloth (7)	164
Daniel Challis (9)	165
Lauren Morley (9)	165
Macaulay Harrison (8)	166

The Westborough Primary School, Westcliff-on-Sea

Matthew Seman (8)	166
Anastasia Chinery (10)	167
Natasha Stone (10)	167
Helena Layzell (8)	168
Lauren Fryer (10)	168
Jack Quy (8)	169
Alex Jones (11)	169
Hollian Gibbs-Leake (8)	170
Rachel Ellis (8)	171
Benjamin Cooper (9)	171
Jade Butler (9)	172
Megan Said	172
Poppy Aubrey (8)	172
Josh Mendes (8)	173
William Summers (8)	173
Joseph Jordan (8)	173
Shannon Dorrington (8)	174
Charles Deebank (8)	174
Caroline Howe (9)	174
Tanaka Mutonono (11)	175
Emmanuel Gbegli (11)	175

Sam Sage (10)	176
Rachael King (11)	176
Emily Summers (10)	177
Samantha Harrold (8)	177
Louis Hosking (8)	178
Joshua Ross (10)	178
Alexander Turpin (11)	179
Emma Davies (11)	179
Katrina Wakeling (10)	180
Justine Jefferies (11)	180
Luke Savidge (11)	181
Robert Heathcote (11)	181
James Middleton (10)	182
Lydia Ellis (10)	182
Gemma Larking (11)	183
Carrie Beckett (11)	183
Alex Lawrence (11)	184
Nicole Drumm (11)	184
Rebecca Johnson (11)	185
Tom Hawkyard (11)	185
Latoya Smith (10)	186
Waleed Moerat (11)	186
Katherine Ridley (11)	187
Ashley Webb (11)	188
Jordan Hixon (11)	188
Tony Norton	189
Carl Ashbrook (11)	189
Kevin Lavery (11)	190
Simone Porter (11)	190
Rose-Marie Forward (10)	191
James Querney (11)	191
Massie Mutonono (11)	192
Catherine Roffey (11)	192
Max Piper (11)	193
Dean Butt (10)	194
Elliot Huxtable (10)	194

Walgrave CP School, Northampton

Lloyd Mallison (8)	194
Florence Neilson (9)	195
Iola McCorkindale (9)	195

Alex McCorkindale (9)	195
Sofia Bonsor (10)	195
Ben Tout (9)	196
Steven Percival-Clare (10)	196
Laura Beckett (10)	196
Holly Bell (10)	196
Laura Howes (8)	197
Katie Worthington (10)	197

Winchester House School, Brackley

Juliet Sparrow (9)	197
Alice Wood (10)	198
Sophie Scott (10)	199
James Rudkin (9)	199
Tabitha Owen (10)	200
Georgia Mossman (10)	201
Ned Kingdon (9)	202
Oscar Cole (10)	202
Sarah Warner (10)	203
Charlie Winton (10)	204
Joe Tusting (10)	205
Emily Taylor (9)	206
Ben Strong (10)	207
Archie Smyth-Osbourne (10)	208
Alex Smith (10)	209
Ben Seymour	210
Lucinda Sewell (10)	211
Pierre Scrase (10)	212
Ned Rodger (10)	213
Alexander Burns (10)	214
Sam Pointon (10)	214
Emily Marchant (10)	215
Polly Mainds (10)	216
Tom Lynas (10)	217
Sophie Lees-Millais (10)	218
Philip Hart (9)	219
Michael Evans (10)	220
Siobhan Dick (9)	221
Louis de Watteville (9)	222
Emma Crawfurd (9)	223
Alex Comfort	224

William Clarke (10) 225
Rowan Brogden (10) 226
James Bowden (10) 227
Florence Cain 228
Harriett Clitheroe (11) 229

Woodton CP School, Bungay
Emily Ratcliffe (9) 229
Kai Garrett (10) 230
Ben Walker (9) 230
Hannah Tynan (11) 230
Jamie Ellis (8) 231
Tara Constable (9) 231
Rachel McAvilley (7) 232
Emily Todd (10) 232
Gareth Bush (10) 232
Lauren Seely (10) 233
Bethany Havers (10) 233
Zoë Ratcliffe (11) 234
Gemma Clutten (8) 234

The Poems

Taste Spring

Taste spring in the park
Where flowers are shooting open and shining.
Taste spring in the garden
Where the frogs are jumping.

Taste spring in the church
Where new babies are christened.
Taste spring in the field
Where the lambs are skipping in the long grass.

Taste spring in the forest
Where buds burst and look at the sun.
Taste spring everywhere,
Where all things grow and come alive.

Alex Cook (7)

The Demolition

Powerful, fearless creature
Tore the delicate classroom apart,
Collapsing like a seagull
Falling from the light blue sky,
Glass shattered like a plate being smashed on the ground,
Walls were rumbling, miraculously like a boxer
Punching through flimsy cardboard,
Two dilapidated mobiles crashing down, like a piece
Of toast crumbling.
An amazing sight,
Fond memories remain forever
Ancient memories destroyed and broken.

Ryan Cammack (10)

The Rocking Reds

Red is the hottest of them all.
Red can be a volcano with
Lava firing down the sides.
Red could also be volcanic ash
Imagine,
Volcanic ash burning
Down everything in its path,
Red is red sandstone
Which the Egyptians made their
Pyramids with.
Red is a warning and an
Alert to stop cars and lorries from crashing!
(Ka boom!)
Red makes me smile
I like being happy.
Red could be the dying of blood
Like this part of the poem.

Rory Kelham (9)

Sunset Funset!

I'm walking on the beach,
My feet sinking in the soft sand,
The water's like a leech, splashing at my hands.
I'm sitting on the rocks, relaxed watching the sunset,
Oh! It's so beautiful, a photo I wish I could get.
The palm trees swaying slowly by the warm, calming breeze,
It's so gorgeous here,
It's impossible to freeze.
I'm going home now,
Wish I could stay,
But I'll always remember the beach that made my day.

Chantelle Ampomah (11)

How Can I Cope!

I have an ambition
Which is big and rough
But I have to reach it
Even if it's tough.

Saving people's lives
Is what I'll try to do
But right now I am suffering
From all the work I have to do.

My exams are coming
Nearer and nearer
But I can't do anything
It's just not fair.

Some people are rude to me
Some are not
But I have to cope
With what I've got.

I wish I had friends
Which are always kind to me
And which treat me well
Just like it's meant to be.

Right now I will cope with what I have got
But sooner or later
Things will change
But I am still happy with what I've got.

Aisha Iqbal (12)

The Writer Of This Poem
(Based on 'The Writer of This Poem' by Roger McGough)

The writer of this poem is . . .
As big as a monster
As small as a hamster
As round as a wedding ring.

The writer of this poem is . . .
As silly as can be
Thinking that after eight years
Her dream might just come true

The writer of this poem . . .
Has a dream to fulfil
A dream to meet Buffy
The one who saved the
    World!

Stephanie Martin (11)

Spiders

Spider, spider
Creeping up the wall,
Spider, spider,
Big and small.

Hairy ones, scary ones,
Eight legs each,
If you see one
It will make you screech.

Spiders are
Everywhere,
Spiders on the floor,
Spiders are
Everywhere,
Crawling on the door.

Rebecca Richards (9)

Big Baby

There once was a laddie
Who slept with his daddy,
And sucked his thumb all day.
He wore a bib
While still in his crib
For eating macaroni.

When his mum put his food on a plate,
He threw it back with hate.
'I don't like this!' he shouted,
So it was off to bed where he pouted,
While the other family knew about it!

'I can't stand this,' said his mum
As the rest of the family were being glum . . .

He's been doing this since he was two
And now he's twenty-two!

Roddy Macrae (11)

Sunshine

S ometimes it is hot
U nless the clouds are out
N ever sit in the sun without
S uncream on
H appy are the children
I n their gardens playing
N ever getting tired
E asily amused.

Nathan Heels (10)

The Cheetah

Its erect ears and its prowling eyes
Search for its prey in an endless disguise.

Its long sleek body, ready to pounce,
When an innocent creature reveals itself.

Out of the long grass the cheetah will dart
And insert its jaw in the creature's heart.

Olivia Ireson (11)

A Riddle

I practically have four legs and eyes.
I could be a bed but not very often.
If someone saw me it could damage their eyes.
I've been in the wars with a lot of my kind.

What am I?

Answer: A car.

Ilan Strul (11)

Haiku

Going down the steps
I see a wee old blind man
Chasing his shadow.

Aaron Kelly (7)

Dreams – My Sweetie Land

Candy canes in trees
Honeysuckle bees
White chocolate buttercups
Delicious beyond belief

Winders whirling
Caramel swirling
Candyfloss floating on air

Peardrops like raindrops
Sun shining through
A rainbow of colours
To tempt me and you

Streams full of chocolate
Flow through the land
Marshmallow bushes
Picked by hand

Am I in Heaven?
Is this a dream?
The most wonderful sight
You have ever seen.

Harriet Walsh (10)
Aberdour School, Tadworth

Special Day

My special day is my birthday.
This day makes me feel glad and happy,
I wake in the morning to find presents and cards,
My family all sing and we have a good laugh.
It's great to be one year older,
I'll soon be as big as my brother!
There are now more candles to blow out on my cake,
I take a big puff and hope my wish will come true.
Cake, presents and lots of fun,
My birthday really is a special day.

Ben Smith (9)
Aberdour School, Tadworth

The Foxes

The fox is waiting all the day,
Waiting for his tasty prey.
The fox is watching through the night,
Waiting for the deadly fight.

The fox is in his darkened den,
Watching for a chicken or hen.

Then he sees a man with a gun,
The man then shoots, the fox he'll run.
The fox has a wife and children following behind,
What scary things must be going through his mind!

They then come to a dead end,
The fox decides he has to defend,
The fox distracts the aggressive man,
While the foxes run out, into more land.

The foxes run and then the male,
The man follows but later he'll fail,
They wriggle under some barbed wire,
All the man can do is stand and fire.

All the foxes got away,
But at that point they were the prey!

Camilla Shopland (10)
Aberdour School, Tadworth

Summer

Summer days come to stay
Winter clouds go away
Sitting by the ripe hot sun
Drinking Coke and having fun

Summer is my favourite time
Up and down the dunes I climb
Down in Dorset by the sea
I am as happy as can be.

Sam Boulton (9)
Aberdour School, Tadworth

Run Away Fox

Run away fox,
Please don't stop,
If you stop,
You'll get shot!

Run away fox,
Don't hide in that box.
The dogs will smell you,
Then what will you do?

Run away fox,
The hounds are almost here,
Oh dear, oh dear,
Can you feel the fear?

Run away fox,
Run for your life!
Get back to your wife,
And live a life?

Jessica Scholfield (9)
Aberdour School, Tadworth

Summer

My birthday's in June
And the flowers start to bloom
All the plants grow
Ice creams start to flow
Day trips to the seaside is what I like best
It's good to run around just in my vest
Rushing through the sprinkler when it's very hot
Sunflower's growing in a pot
I like the summer it's really cool
Sitting in the garden in my paddling pool.

Jack Cotsworth (8)
Aberdour School, Tadworth

Summer Breeze

Winter is over! Winter is over!
No more frostbite, colds and flu
Hello warmness, fun and sun.

Summer breeze come to stay
June, July, August
Oh I wish 'twas here in May.

Now we come out to play!
Kites flying into the sky
We see planes go by.

But we don't want the time to fly
Oh I wish the summer breeze would stay
More, forever our way.

Daniel Coppen (10)
Aberdour School, Tadworth

The Fox

This night, a calm night,
Brings with it the fox.
Its long bushy tail
Brushes over the grass.

It sleeps in the day
Comes out in the night.
Its orange-red colour
With its gleaming eyes.

Making it easy to see,
But only in England.
With the bright green grass,
Not in Australia with its dusty plains.

It is the Red Fox.

Jacob Ansell (11)
Aberdour School, Tadworth

The Fox

I pounce around mostly at night,
Catching rabbits in my flight

Which I gobble up as quickly as I can,
Before I'm caught by that monster called Man

And part of my day is often spent looking through
The household bins

Where I find amazing things hidden in rusty old
Tins

I also like the occasional hen,
Which I usually catch from the farmer's men

But when they see me they grab their guns
And I begin a desperate run

At last I see a glance of my den

I think I'll make it with the hen

Then I am suddenly chased round and round
By a pack of hungry hounds

I am sprinting for the finishing line,
Yes I'll make it just in time.

Ben Wackett (9)
Aberdour School, Tadworth

The Fox

At night he comes out
All ready to catch his prey -
Cats, mice, squirrels and rabbits
He lays in the dark until his prey comes
He sees what he wants and he pounces . . .
He pierces the animal's throat
And drags it into
His den.

Alex Wade (10)
Aberdour School, Tadworth

Dreams

My eyes are closed,
My room is dark,
It's time to dream,
Vanilla, chocolate or strawberry ice cream.

My pony is chestnut with dark brown eyes,
I trot around the field,
And win every prize.

I'm in an adventure park,
Racing along at a very fast speed,
I'm now holding hands with a gorilla,
I'm about to feed.

I open my eyes,
In comes the light,
What will be in my dreams by tonight.

Hannah Pipe (10)
Aberdour School, Tadworth

Dreams!

I dream of making beautiful dresses
For pop stars, models and actresses
I would also make a lot for me
That's just one of the things I'd like to be

I dream of being in a salon doing hair
Changing colours and hairstyles with such care
My hair would be especially nice to see
That's just one of the things I'd like to be

I dream of being a manicurist and painting people's nails
Some would be painted bright red and others just pale
My own nails will be pink with bright white tops
So many dreams, I can't wait to grow up!

Sophia Syed (9)
Aberdour School, Tadworth

Summer

The grass is growing lush,
And there are people in a rush,
Summer holidays have just begun,
And we're all having fun.

The sun is in the sky,
And birds are flying high,
Summer holidays have just begun,
And nature's having fun.

The children are a screaming,
And the hosepipes are a teeming,
Summer holidays have just begun,
And children are having fun.

The flowers are a blooming,
And the trees are a blowing,
Summer holidays have just begun,
And flowers are having fun.

Now the grass has finished growing,
And back to work we're going,
Summer holidays are all done,
And put an end to all that fun.

The sun is going down,
And the birds are in a frown,
Summer holidays are all done,
Nature's missing all the fun.

The summer holidays may be done,
But there's much more fun to come,
As the weekend's on its way,
And we'll all have time to play.

Emma Ward (10)
Aberdour School, Tadworth

Summer

Oooooohh, I love those long hot summer days,
To enjoy the sun in many different ways.

Playing cricket on the village green,
On the beach eating ice cream.

Off to Cornwall we go camping,
Eating all those Cornish pasties.

When I go and play with friends,
We hate it when our fun ends.

At the seaside we see boats,
Watching all those swimmers float.

Summer evenings long and cool,
Barbecuing by the pool.

Going to theme parks with rides whizzing round,
Children screaming with delight, as they go upside down.

People sunbathing in the garden,
Listening to music and having fun.

Oh no! the summer's ended,
Now it's back to school to see my friends.

Thomas Hornsey (10)
Aberdour School, Tadworth

Moods

Sometimes I feel happy.
Sometimes I feel sad.
Sometimes I feel angry.
Sometimes I feel mad.
Sometimes I feel silly.
Sometimes I feel bad.
Sometimes I feel good.
It depends upon my mood.

Thomas Bradbury (8)
Aberdour School, Tadworth

The Fox

Sly, quiet and quick Mister Fox

My eyes are so tired,
I hide away all day.
My tummy is rumbling.
As the sun goes down
And the stars come out to play.

My eyes are so bright
When I prowl at night.
As I visit the hen house
And give them a fright
When I take a bite!

Then I have to run
Before the farmer comes
With his pump action shot gun!
Back to my den in the country
For a day's rest before the night.

Adam Creswell (8)
Aberdour School, Tadworth

Dreams

I dream of flying in the air,
Lying on a soft white cloud.
Feel the air blowing through my hair,
And feel no ground beneath my feet.
I'd see angels flying everywhere
And talk to everyone that I meet.
I dream of living there,
And have wings instead of feet.
I live in a palace made of pink fluff
No windows or doors just an open roof.
Oh no there's the alarm clock here comes Mum!

Laura Sharman (11)
Aberdour School, Tadworth

The School Trip

Are we here? Yes we are! Where are we?
On a star of course!
Wow it's shiny and glittery - like the moon.
Whoa it's a martian coming to greet us
To its foreign land. It's giving us a sweet
Hot! Hot! Hot!
It was a chilli banger.
Here comes the fireworks.

It is nearly night.
The hunters are coming
Back from their hunt and doing their kung fu.
Bash, boom, bang, wallop
They've fallen over - what a shame
We have to leave
They are giving us chocolates and a rest.
They said 'We thank you for visiting our land'
And then left.

Harry Ellison (8)
Aberdour School, Tadworth

The Pop Star

One day I dream of being a star
Singing and dancing are my passion in my car.
They would hear my songs across the lands
Oh so far.
One day I dream of being a star.
In my bedroom and in the bath,
I sing so loud it flies to the clouds.
One day I dream of being a star
I just want to be a pop star.

Megan Brockman (9)
Aberdour School, Tadworth

The Fox

I can hear the fox hunt, the fox hunt
I can hear the horses pounding right on my tail
I can hear the dogs growling, the dogs growling
I can hear the men shouting as they look for me.

Am I hiding in the bushes or down low in the grass?
Can the dogs smell me out?
They are fast but I am quicker
I have found a hole in the ground.

The dogs are near
I can feel their breath and smell them
They have almost found me
But then their masters call them away.

I am still free to see my family
I have escaped them today
Next time they may catch me
But that day will have to wait . . .

Oliver Reavley (9)
Aberdour School, Tadworth

The School Trip

Waiting, waiting for the bus to come,
There I see it,
Are we there yet Mum?
Now we're at the farm with the ducks and geese,
But look in my lunch box it's packed full of sweets!
Wow, look at those horses having a rest,
And those annoying chickens are being a real pest.
Boo! We're going home that was real fun
My friend Dave agrees, he thinks it's dumb
Waiting, waiting for the bus to go,
Hey wait a minute, I have another sweet to go!

Joshua Morris (9)
Aberdour School, Tadworth

Dreams

Oh how I like my glorious dreams
Tennis, football anything I like.
I had some dreams I won anything that stood in my way.
Football, every league, every tournament
Is passed with the glorious feeling of,
Winning!
My wonderful dreams.

Oh how I like my glorious dreams
Tennis, football anything I like.
I had some dreams I won anything that stood in my way
Tennis I won the matches, tournaments and best of all Grand Slams.
And it's all passed with the glorious feeling of
Winning!
My wonderful dreams.

Ollie Batchelor (10)
Aberdour School, Tadworth

The Hungry Fox

The hungry fox was looking for prey,
Standing on a barrel of hay.
Searching for his daily meal,
He saw a chicken he would steal.

He crept up quietly, looking around
Then pounced, knocking the chicken to the ground.
Lots of squawking, feathers everywhere
The fox carried on, he didn't care.

Chewing on the bloody flesh,
Which tasted nice, it tasted fresh.
He munched until he'd had his fill,
Then slipped away from the scene of the kill.

Christopher Gee (10)
Aberdour School, Tadworth

Special Day

I enter the Taverner's stand
The pavilion to my left looks grand
I find my usual seat
A bright sun gives off lots of heat.

The crowd are eagerly awaiting the day
A loud clapping and cheering before play,
After the teams enter the pitch
The first over goes without a hitch.

One team fields and one team bats
The batsmen all wear safety hats,
Lots of runs and wickets are taken
My team are losing so I am shaken.

Lords is the best place for cricket
There is more than one excellent wicket,
The outfield is green and fast
The ground has an amazing past.

Antony Kalindjian (11)
Aberdour School, Tadworth

Summer

S ummer days are long
U pward heat shines down
M errily we play in the garden 'til late
M aybe we'll have our dinner outside
E vening never seems to end
R ainy days spoil our fun but,

D ays to come bring more sun
A round us happiness is here once again
Y ou must come and join our fun
S ometime soon while summer fun lasts.

Eiméar Monaghan (9)
Aberdour School, Tadworth

Summer

The sun is hot and beats down,
The pool is inviting,
We jump in and make a splash,
You hit the bottom and go bash.

Mum's shouting it's time to eat,
Can't be bothered just sit on the seat.
'Let's have a drink I only want Coke,'
I'm not allowed, it makes me choke.

The food's on the table,
The BBQ's red-hot,
I'll take a chance and sit on the floor,
I hope the ants don't get there before.

Back in the pool,
The water's so cool,
We have lots of fun
Being out in the sun.

It's time to dry and get dressed,
The breeze is up and it's getting cold.
We pack our things and go home,
And wait for another summer's day.

Matthew Van-Noort-Pendleton (8)
Aberdour School, Tadworth

Summer Days

Summer days are warm and sunny
Play outside with my mummy.

                Winter days are wet and grey
                Have to stay in all day.

Summer days are blue and bright
Spent on the beach seems so right.

                Winter days are snowy and cold
                Only go outside if you're bold!

Gregory Hodgson (8)
Aberdour School, Tadworth

Moods

Moods are very unusual things,
They just decide to go and come.
Moods can make your feelings change,
Feel happy, sad or glum.

Sometimes I feel sad and hurt,
Because of what people say or do.
When this happens I sometimes cry,
I feel bad and don't know what to do.

When I am happy I feel so good,
And am always full of joy.
I like to be happy most of all,
Because there's nothing I don't enjoy.

Sometimes when I am feeling silly,
I mess around and play.
And these are my main moods,
That I feel throughout the day.

Alex Huber (11)
Aberdour School, Tadworth

Dreams

Every night I go to sleep
Every night I dream a dream.
Sometimes they're good
Sometimes they're bad.
Sometimes they're happy
Sometimes they're sad.
Sometimes I'm chasing monsters
Sometimes I'm slaying dragons.
But all in all it's still just a dream
And not really real!

Oliver Robinson (11)
Aberdour School, Tadworth

The School Trip

I love to be with all my friends
On a special school trip that never ends

We have such fun on our old school bus
Looking, chatting is a must!

Where will our journey end
In this village or around this bend?

Castles, gardens, museums, Victorian schools we must see
As we jump up and down on the bus with glee.

These trips are special on any day
Looking, learning, as we go on our merry way

I will never forget this precious time
As we hop off the bus in an orderly line.

Rebecca Mullett (9)
Aberdour School, Tadworth

My Special Day

I wake up in the morning feeling very fine
Today will be the day I'll have a great time
I'm off on holiday to sunny Spain
We're going from Gatwick on an aeroplane
We're going to go swimming, play golf and tennis
We're taking my little sister and she's a bit of a menace
As soon as I get there I'm going to jump in the sea
Then we'll go to the restaurant for an enormous big tea
Every morning I'll go to my golf lessons at the range
The pro's name is Martin, he's a bit strange
We'll stay there for a week, having a wonderful time
I'll go back again when I am nine.

James Barlow (9)
Aberdour School, Tadworth

Dreams

I'm in a world of my own,
In a country of my own,
In a city of my own,
In a town of my own.

Where bluebirds are pink,
And goldfish are green,
Where oranges are yellow,
And peaches are blue.

Where I can be free,
Scream and shout,
Run about,
Jump up and down.

Where I can eat Chinese, Cantonese,
Peking and Indian,
Traditional English,
Or just a plain bacon sandwich.

Where I eat pineapples, kiwis,
Pears, apples, or cherries,
Where I can eat cakes and ice cream,
Sweeties and chocolate.

But then my alarm goes,
And Mum comes to wake me up!

Jessica Kay-Ogunsola (11)
Aberdour School, Tadworth

The School Trip

The school trip,
School trip
We all go on a school trip.
But in the morning
I woke up,
But it was rain,
It was a bit of a pain.

Early next morning
We all went to Kew Gardens
I thought it might have been better for the flower.

The day we went was the best day
All the flowers were in the best moods
We were in our best moods
As well as the flowers.
So beautiful as a sky
I even thought it was only a colour.
Even the tulips were down a little bit,
The colour was nice red,
With a little drop of water.
The other flowers were also nice.

I knew,
The rain made the flowers go very beautiful.
Thank you rain.

Naohiro Hattori (10)
Aberdour School, Tadworth

Dreams

Winter dreams of snowfall chilling,
Accompanied by the frostbite freezing,
Jack Frost will come out to play,
Every morning of each day.

Autumn dreams of oak leaves brown,
Just outside our busy town,
Conkers on strings and other things,
Make this season a fun little fling.

Spring dreams of blossom on the trees,
A sight which often brings me to my knees,
Oh how I wish I cold spend all my days,
In the months of March, April and May.

Summer dreams of red hot sun,
And fun being had by everyone,
Playing in the sand and splashing in the water,
Everyone is sad that this season will falter.

Ben Aldersley (11)
Aberdour School, Tadworth

Dream

I dream of playing for England, in my cricket whites.
On hot summer days and balmy summer nights.
No rain would stop my play, when bowling
Down the crease.
I'd catch those batsmen out! 'How's that?'
I'd shout.
And every match we would win and bring the
Ashes back,
Oh I wish I could captain the England team
That is my very greatest dream.

James Saunders (9)
Aberdour School, Tadworth

The Fox

In the mornings you wake up,
You see the wonderful sun,
But at the corner of your eye,
You see some bits of rubbish,
Bins over,
Who's to blame?

At night you see them,
Come out of their territory,
And come round sniffing.

Who's this devil?
Tipping our bins,
And getting in our way,
I'll tell you who it is,
Mr Fox.

Kiran Govekar (11)
Aberdour School, Tadworth

Dreams

When I'm lying asleep in bed,
My dream for the night creeps into my head.

In most of my dreams I'm happy and glad,
But in some of them I'm very sad.

I am either eating a delicious ice cream,
Or my dream is scary so I scream.

When I run to my mum and say I had a nightmare
She gives me a hug and says there, there.

And when my mum puts me back into bed,
Another dream finds its way into my head.

Zoe Rutherford (11)
Aberdour School, Tadworth

Dream Of Becoming A Policeman

When I go to bed at night,
I dream of becoming a policeman,
I dream of wearing a policeman's hat,
And driving in a squad car.

I'd gather up all the robbers,
And put them all in jail,
I'd make sure all the people on the streets are safe,
By having a sneak and prowl.

So while I'm about,
Just watch out,
Captain Harry's,
On his shout.

Harry Carpenter (10)
Aberdour School, Tadworth

Dreams

Some nights my sleep is dreamless
Others are sleeping adventures
In some dreams I am fearless
In others my nana takes out her dentures!

Some nights I dream of fast cars
In others I am a football star
Some nights I am living on Mars
Others are just for laughs.

Some dreams make me smile
Others make me sigh
Some dreams go on for miles
While others leave me high and dry.

Sam Adams (8)
Aberdour School, Tadworth

Moods

Good moods, bad moods
Happy and sad moods.

Good moods make me
Smile at the sunshine,
I'm chirpy like a bird,
I'm carefree on top of the world.
I whistle in the sunshine,
I'm happy, I'm laughing,
I'm glad, not sad.

Bad moods put me down in the dumps,
All gloomy and sad,
I'm miserable and fed up,
I think I'm going mad.

My face wears a frown,
I'm feeling really down,
I'm cross and I'm snappy,
I'd much rather be happy.

Jamie Beard (10)
Aberdour School, Tadworth

Dreams

Dreams are like sensations, you always feel them.
They come in all shapes and sizes, colours like red and blue.
The moment your eyelids drop a new world opens up.
You could step inside your fantasy or hide from the world.
Every night a new door opens, you never know which.
But you dare to look inside for the surprise that might lie within.
But then you wake up to the sound of your clock!
Just before you reached the special door.
But don't worry there's no need to hurry.
You'll be back there soon enough.
With your memories in your head, from the last night in your bed.

Natasha Moore (11)
Aberdour School, Tadworth

The Fiendish Fox

The fox is fast,
It goes like a blast.
It catches its prey,
In night and day,
It rummages through bins,
And gets stuck in tins.
It hurries away
It's almost day.

The fiendish fox,
Jumped into a box.
The box was carried away,
But the fox wanted to stay.
He popped his head up high,
It almost touched the sky,
First to come out
Was the snout
Of the *fiendish fox*.

There, everywhere,
Here and there.
Lock up carefully,
They're not trustworthy
Look after your weans,
They'll give them pains.
So in the night,
You might get a fright,
Because of *the fiendish fox*.

Calum Watt (10)
Aberdour School, Tadworth

Christmas Day

On Christmas Day I wake up early
I get out of bed and feel all twirly,
I run downstairs and meet my dad,
He looks as if he's going mad.

I go and open all my presents,
I've got a Game Boy and a chess set,
My sister's got a big, pink doll's house,
And she has a big, fat white mouse.

After I've opened all my presents,
We go and get my gran and grandad,
We bring them home and sit them down,
But they want to have a good look round.

For lunch we have roast turkey and potatoes,
I've spilt the gravy on my trousers,
I go upstairs and get them washed,
My mum comes up and tells me off.

It's been a lovely day,
But now it's getting late,
'It's time to go to bed,' says Mum,
And that's the bit I hate!

Guy Lester (9)
Aberdour School, Tadworth

Dreams

Last night I dreamt I was a dragon,
The night before I was a cat,
I dream of family,
I dream of friends,
I dream of good things and of bad,
Sometimes I dream of holidays,
And sometimes I even dream that there is an alien attack,
Now I wonder what I will be tonight,
I'll just have to wait and see.

Connie Woollen (10)
Aberdour School, Tadworth

The School Trip

In the coach going nowhere,
Boogers are flying everywhere.

We get to the zoo,
And I saw a kangaroo.
The gorilla was hairy,
But not very bright.
The lions are angry,
I don't want to be in their fight.

The cheetah is running
Look at her go,
Really fast, not now slow.
And look at the antelopes,
Trying to get away.

A big snake, a python I think,
Made a large stink.
The gas was so vast,
That it blew up a vase.

As we went home
Well I can't say
I will tell you one thing
That we were kicked out of the zoo for sure!

James Pine (9)
Aberdour School, Tadworth

Summer

I love summer it's lovely and calm,
Unlike winter which there is always an alarm.
I love summer you're always bold,
Unlike winter because you're always cold.
I love summer it's lovely and warm,
Unlike spring when there is always a storm.
I love summer it's always sunny,
Unlike winter because it's always snowy.

Callum White (11)
Aberdour School, Tadworth

Summer

You know that summer's here when . . .
Birds begin to sing,
Flowers start to bloom,
Long happy days, children playing in the sun.

You know that summer's here when . . .
Rainy days are few,
Butterflies flutter through,
Friends meet up and enjoy barbecues.

You know that summer's here when . . .
Beach days are here,
Sandcastles start to appear,
Long summer days - happy, happy memories.

Sophie Ayles (8)
Aberdour School, Tadworth

Dreams

I dream, I dream of lots of things,
I dream, I dream of a cat with wings,
When I dream I get taken away,
Taken away to a fun place to play.

I dream, I dream of having a wish,
And using that wish to be a fish.
In my dreams I go anywhere
Sometimes I go to see a bear.

When I wake up my dreams go away
Away until the end of today.

Daniel Godden (11)
Aberdour School, Tadworth

Special Day

It's a special day today,
Everybody knows it,
It's a special day today,
See if you know it.

Everyone is dressed in lovely red and white,
And some people also blue,
Lots of people are out flying their kites,
Into the sky immensely blue.

Everyone is cheerful,
For it is a very special day,
Everyone is cheerful,
For it is Saint George's Day!

Alisdair Kemp (11)
Aberdour School, Tadworth

Fox

The fox, the fox, prowling around,
Looking for food and making no sound,
Sniffing 'round dustbins, desperate for food,
Five hungry cubs, no time to lose!

There's ice on the ground, no water to drink,
The fox carries on, it's all very bleak,
Morning approaches, light appears in the skies,
She goes back to the den to hide from our eyes.

Now summer approaches, her coat is more sleek,
As cunning as ever, she dares food to seek,
It's up to the fields, she slinks to the farm,
Her shrieks fill the air, all is not calm!

Matthew Ayles (11)
Aberdour School, Tadworth

The School Trip

The school trip was fun,
We sat on a coach,
We went past the seaside,
And told silly jokes.
We drove past the golf course
And saw a man putt,
We walked past the farm
And saw a rabbit in a hutch.
We stopped to have lunch,
What a nice day it's been
We've all had great fun,
The best I've ever seen.

Samuel Lee (11)
Aberdour School, Tadworth

Summer

Spring is over
Summer is beginning
A blue sky with a yellow warm sun
There are children running
Because they're having fun
In the park, under the sun
Red ladybirds with black dots
Dance in the shade
Bees are buzzing, taking pollen from flowers
Sunflowers grow tall and sway in the breeze
Autumn is a long way away.

Thomas Eades (8)
Aberdour School, Tadworth

The Fox

The fox was in our garden chewing, sniffing stuff.
Once he destroyed and ate our flip flops . . .
He went through our garbage, eating our rubbish!
Once he even ate my dog's dinner when we were watching . . .

That fox is crazy, it eats absolutely everything . . .
What do I do if my mum and dad catch it?
They'll probably keep it as a pet – those crazy,
Crazy parents of mine!

Richard Hawkins (11)
Aberdour School, Tadworth

My Mouse Can Go Bowling

My mouse can go bowling
My mouse can wrestle with a man
My mouse can shave his beard
My mouse is called Dan.

My mouse can drive rockets
My mouse can grow his bones big
My mouse can do a flip
My mouse can eat like a pig.

Sebastian Patrick (6)
Ashdon CP School, Saffron Walden

Snow

Snow is white, snow is bright, snow is a big fright.
When we get home we have cold feet, we have our supper
And we go to our bed to sleep.
When we get up the snow is still there
We do not know where to go
But we are still there.

Amy Longmore (10)
Crathes Primary School, Banchory

A World Without Trees

A world without trees is chaos,
We'd never live for ninety years,
Everyone would have loss of oxygen,
And life would not carry on.

The birds would fall from their nests
And the shrews would have no homes
Monkeys would have nothing to climb
And the squirrels would have no food.

We know that trees give us oxygen
So the big cats would fall to the ground,
Elephants would faint and die
Oh what would we do without trees?

A world without trees is chaos
We'd never live for ninety years,
Everyone would have loss of oxygen
And life would not carry on.

Darren McLuskie (10)
Dalry Primary School, Edinburgh

War!

Every day people die
Some laugh, some cry.
British running to their den
Hitler sending all his men.
Italy, France, Russia and Spain
Each one had their own campaign.
Winston Churchill shouting orders
Fighting Germans on his borders.
Hitler is finally dead
He took a bullet in the head.

David Glass (11)
Dalry Primary School, Edinburgh

A World Without Trees

Imagine a world without trees . . .

Trees give us oxygen
So that we can breathe,
Trees give us paper
To write on or draw,
Trees give us fruit
To keep us healthy and fit.

What about the animals?
They'll have no shelter
To hide from the cold,
Where will they live?
They'll have nowhere to go . . .

We'll never hear the rustling of leaves,
We'll never see the blossoms in spring,
Imagine a world without trees . . .

Kandice Wood (10)
Dalry Primary School, Edinburgh

A World Without Trees

Trees falling apart like rusty metal,
Whispering frantically through the wind,
Having no leaves or branches,
No fruits for people to eat,
No oxygen in the air,
No wood or twigs to burn,
Hearing no noises through the trees
Lonely without solid trees,
Trees lying about with crumpled leaves
Gazing through the strong wind,
No homes for animals to stay,
No twigs to twist to make a nest,
Echoes from the empty forest
I can't imagine a world without trees . . .

Farhan Ali (10)
Dalry Primary School, Edinburgh

The Beach

I see the sun setting
I smell the fresh air
I hear the ocean's roar
I feel the sinking sand
I taste coconuts
I'm in a lucky place.

Natanya Feeley (10)
Ferguslie Primary School, Paisley

The Cup Final

The fans are cheering for me.
The excitement of the match
The whistle of the referee
The gold cup in my hands
The goals of courage did it
We've won the gold cup.

Jamie Skalley (10)
Ferguslie Primary School, Paisley

Pirate Land

The pirate that's staring at me
The sea that's covering the land
The moans of the pirates
The sword that's on me
The sword that's cutting my throat
That's the end of me.

Jordan Foster (9)
Ferguslie Primary School, Paisley

Heaven's Wonder

The golden gates of Heaven
The beautiful smell of perfume
The sweet sound of birds singing
The soft clouds under my feet
The lovely taste of my favourite sweet
I'm being carried away with Cupid's angels.

Lauren McPhee (9)
Ferguslie Primary School, Paisley

The Fabulous Beach

The waves tumbling onto the rocks
The seaweed and the lovely sand
The shells making sounds of the water
The cold breaths of wind blowing
The ice cream and delicious candyfloss
The beach is a lovely place for children.

Nicola Moran (9)
Ferguslie Primary School, Paisley

Disneyland

Roller coasters behind my back
Juice and tea
Rides going boom, boom, boom
So full of joy
Dust from old little rides
I'll go back some day.

Lisa Humphries (9)
Ferguslie Primary School, Paisley

My Ten Pets

I have ten pets
They're really mad
When they go to the vets
It makes me sad.

My dog's called Bill
And my cat's named Ben
My pig's called Jill
And my cow's named Den.

I have some reptiles
They're wonderful,
My snake's called Matt
And my chameleon Pat.

Rats are horrible
But mine are friendly
My male's named Lou
And the female Sue.

I have two young guinea pigs
They're nice and cuddly
The black one's called Greg
And the brown one's named Fred.

My pets are amazing
I love them to bits,
I'm glad that I got them
For me they're big hits.

Matthew Furniss (11)
Knaphill Junior School, Woking

Hear Me Out

I do believe
You annoy me
You take my shoe
And graze my knee!

You take my key,
You ignore me
Even though
You hear my plea!

I do believe
You bully me
You always hurt me
Stop you bully!

Ben Howes (11)
Knaphill Junior School, Woking

My Bossy Teacher

My bossy teacher
Has snakes in her hair
She roars when she talks
Like no one's there.
Her eyes stick out
Like twigs in the air
This is my bossy teacher
And no one cares.

Priyanka Modgill (11)
Knaphill Junior School, Woking

Fish (And Chickens)

Some fish are white,
Some fish are brown,
As they glide,
As they slide,
Through the water, through the water.

Some bite their fin,
Some quite like gin,
As they glide,
As they slide,
Through the water, through the water.

Even though my fish are great,
I really wish I had a mate,
That is why I want a chicken,
Even though all they do is peck,
I still wish I could break their neck,
(Very tasty with some gravy).

Ellie Bostock (11)
Knaphill Junior School, Woking

Dolphins

They swim beautifully
Around in the sea
Wild, careless and free.

They jump and spin,
With a flick of a fin,
But make sure they're back for tea.

Dolphins are cheerful,
So the sea isn't dull,
And they warm it with their pee.

Chelsea Norman (11)
Knaphill Junior School, Woking

Computer Games

'Great!' you shout when you get a new one
'Amazing!' you shout when you play it
'Mwwarff!' you shout when you lose
Essential for computer-holics
So cool it'll blow your head off!

Fwoosh! The sound when you're racing on it
'Oh no!' you shout when you die . . .
'Rock on!' you shout when you've won
Punch! The characters do on a fighting game
Crash! The cars smash into the wall.
'Super!' you say when you have finished it,
    'Now onto the next game' you say.

Billy Lee (10)
Knaphill Junior School, Woking

Sport

Football is to kick a ball
Into a wild open net
There's a monster blocking the way,
But we'll just call him the goalie.

F1 is to go round and round
It may be boring at first,
But soon there is a crash
That makes the sport so fun.

Rugby is so great,
England are the best,
As they won the World Cup,
Back in November.

Charlie Simms (11)
Knaphill Junior School, Woking

How Beautiful Is The Sun

How beautiful is the sun
After the night has gone
In the sun it shines so bright
In the clouds the sun appears
How beautiful is the sun.

How it shines upon everyone
Like the moon at night
How it moves across the Earth
From the east to the west.

Across the clouds it passed
It is bright as Venus
And comes out every day
With a rise when it comes out
Like spring has gone
The sun is beautiful like everyone.

Riandra Moynihan (11)
Knaphill Junior School, Woking

Holiday Stuff

H aving fun
O ff I go
L iving my life
I love it so
D ay all gone
A gain it will come
Y oghurt and things
   Are so much fun.

S illy sandcastles
T he waves come in
U nited together
F orever
F in.

Lucy Franklin (11)
Knaphill Junior School, Woking

Winter Cold

As I walk through the rain,
It starts to sting my face with pain,
After a while it starts to snow,
And it gives the ground a special glow.
It is cold, but I am bold,
And I walk through it bravely,
For I know, the faster I go
I get home quick and safely.

Shaunii Robb (11)
Knaphill Junior School, Woking

The Seashore

The glistening water sparkles so bright
And the sand is warm from the light
The ice creams are cold
And the shells are green, brown and black
The seagulls screech
That's why I love
The fantastic beach.

Hannah Deluce (11)
Knaphill Junior School, Woking

Riddle

Because I am by nature blind,
I wisely choose to walk behind,
Although my speech is spoke with sense,
All my speaking gives offence
The company will leave the room.

Peter Prince (11)
Knaphill Junior School, Woking

The Creatures

There once was a room filled with lightning
Where creatures were made to start fighting
These creatures had saws
Rear and side doors
And teeth made especially for biting.

The creatures were from a far land
A place with plenty of sand
The creatures got tired
From a cannon they were fired
Which made all their heads expand!

Alex Paterson (11)
Knaphill Junior School, Woking

A Poem About Food

Sausage, mash and beans are my favourite *fab!*
Although apple crumble is the winner
The greasiest of all is fish and chips
But I prefer great Indian curry.

Burgers and cakes so delicious, yum-yum!
Apples and oranges so juicy mmm!
Ice cream and jelly beat the rest oh yeah!
But I want to be fit so fruit and *veg*!

Chris Warburn (11)
Knaphill Junior School, Woking

Ducks

D ucks are cute and sweet
U will be a duck some day
'C ause they are just like you and me
K ind, sweet and little darlings
S ome day they will be cuter.

Katie Winter (11)
Knaphill Junior School, Woking

The Bully

It came across the playground
And then it hit me.
It hit me hard upon the head.
I felt like my whole world had just gone dead.

Then the tears rolled down my face
And all those hated words
Cry-baby, wet-bag and teacher's-pet
They came at me in painful herds.

Laura Cugulliere (11)
Knaphill Junior School, Woking

Animal

A nts travel around the ground
N obody cares about the lives of animals
I nsects take pollen
M ammals live everywhere, they don't hatch from eggs
A nimals come in different shapes, sizes and colours
L azy lions lay around all day.

Kerry Dwan (10)
Knaphill Junior School, Woking

Sport

S occer is a worldwide sport with its own competitions.
P rofessionals carry out all sports well
O lympics are the main sporting event, held every four years.
R unning is a main event at the Olympics
T raining is a main part of becoming a professional.

Sam Smith (11)
Knaphill Junior School, Woking

Summer Breeze

The heat on my face,
The sand in my toes,
The sun on the water,
Makes it sparkle and glow.

The ocean's breeze,
Sprays the birds in the trees
And makes them whistle,
With uncontrolled glee.

The palm trees sway,
On a hot summer's day,
Making everyone feel
Happy and free.

Emma Crampton (11)
Knaphill Junior School, Woking

Adventures

A nimal adventures
D angerous adventures
V acation adventures
E xciting adventures
N asty adventures
T heme park adventures
U rban adventures
R elaxing adventures
E xhausting adventures
S ly adventures

      Adventures are
           Great!

Emma England (11)
Knaphill Junior School, Woking

Fire Rap

Fire is hot, fire is cool
Fire has enough heat, to make you drool.
It sparks you up on a dark cloudy night,
You can't even put it out with a can of Sprite
Fire can cook, any type of food,
Even if you're in an angry mood
Fire is a hot source of burning light
It is good, for giving people a hell of a fright,
And if you don't believe me that fire is the best,
Then put fire to the big almighty test,
So you better fasten your strap
And big leather buckle
But if you don't agree,
You'll face my knuckle.

Oliver Benstead (11)
Knaphill Junior School, Woking

Animals I've Seen

I once saw a cat
And by golly it was fat,
It would jump up and down
Or wag its tail round and round.

I once saw a dog
That was going for a jog
It was barking really loud
And looking at the clouds.

I once saw a rabbit
My mum said 'Quick grab it,'
But the rabbit hopped away
Now what will my mum say?

Charlotte Masson (11)
Knaphill Junior School, Woking

The Killer Wasp

The wasp is flying everywhere
Killing flies in the air
He comes along and eats them up
That's instead of a Pizza Hut
His favourite hobby is to sting
He follows the scent of yummy din
But it's only one jar of jam
And he wishes it was lamb
The wasp takes a gigantic lick
The child looks then he's sick
The wasp sees somebody he doesn't like
Flying straight towards them gives them a fright
He lands on top and gives him a sting
He crouches down and sings
Racing back to his hive he's glad
That he stung Clive!

Steven Pattenden (11)
Knaphill Junior School, Woking

Kittens

K ittens are cute and cuddly
I wish I had them all
T o look after them and treat them well
T o make sure they are safe and sound
E ventually they will turn into cats
N o matter what they do
S omehow I will remember what they looked like
   When they were small.

Leah Partridge (10)
Knaphill Junior School, Woking

My Hobby

My hobby is dancing,
I put on my shoe
Tap, tap, tap,
I think I've got the dance flu.

I dance to the music
The music has beat,
The rhythm of the sound
Takes me off my feet.

I turn off the music
I take off my shoes
But still in my mind
I've still got dance flu.

Emily Laybourn (11)
Knaphill Junior School, Woking

The Dolphins

When the boats are in the sea
And the fish are in the reef
The dolphins are singing a calming song
And jumping out of the sea.
The boats throw nets in the sea
And the fish swim for their lives
The dolphins not knowing the danger
Swim in for a closer look.
Getting tangled in the net trying to break free
The fisherman cuts the net
I'm free, gone back to the sea.

Taylor Shephard (11)
Knaphill Junior School, Woking

My Secret Rapper

My secret rapper
He knows how to rap
He can rock.

He always has the spotlight
Shining on him,
'cause he is da best.

He has muscles
He is strong
He has tattoos.

Can you guess
My secret rapper
Do you want some clues?

He is fit
He has blonde hair
He is da best.

He loves his daughter
His daughter Hayley
His only daughter
His only child
Hayley.

My secret rapper
Who can rock
His name is Eminem.

Daniella White (11)
Knaphill Junior School, Woking

In My House

As I was sat on the couch
My mum screamed out 'Ouch!'
She had sat on a pin,
As my dad stormed in.
'What's up with you?' I said,
As my brother sat sulking in bed,
My sister had been ill,
But still raising the phone bill.

Allana King (11)
Knaphill Junior School, Woking

Growing Up

G rowing up,
R eally isn't much fun,
O ccasionally I get to play,
W hen the time is right you'll get a fright,
I nside I'm getting older and older
N ow I can see how my sister felt . . .
G rowing up!

Amybeth Edwards (11)
Knaphill Junior School, Woking

Horses

H orses eat lots of hay
O ats for snacks any day
R eins and tack
S chool or hack?
E nough of the banter
S how me how to canter!

Elizabeth Biggs (11)
Knaphill Junior School, Woking

My Secret Rapper

My secret rapper
He knows how to rap
He rocks
He always has the spotlight
Because he is da best
He has tattoos on each arm
He has blonde hair
He is fit
Can you guess my secret?
Rapper one more clue
He has a daughter called Hayley
My secret rapper
He can rap
He is Eminem

Eminem is the best!
He rules!

Jess Warwick (11)
Knaphill Junior School, Woking

Food Rap

This is how the food rap goes,
It will tinkle all of your toes,
Cadbury's Rolo, McFlurry,
Or that lovely chicken curry.

Lollies, lollies, everywhere,
You can eat them if you dare,
Even with them lovely roast peas,
Taste nice with the melted cheese.

Bradley Bayliss (11)
Knaphill Junior School, Woking

My Sister's Very Funny

My sister's very funny,
She's really loopy loo,
Sometimes she's really crazy,
You should see what she can do!

She paints with jam from jam pots,
She sings Mozart in the bath,
And when it comes to juggling,
She makes me laugh and laugh!

She's jived with jumping jellyfish
She's touched a porcupine,
She's used a Spanish pencil,
That funny sister of mine!

My sister's very funny,
She's really loopy loo,
Sometimes she's really crazy,
You've heard what she can do!

Naomi Gale (11)
Knaphill Junior School, Woking

Seasons

Spring is the time for reproduction
As newborn lambs skip contentedly around
When heat is around, summer has arrived
Trees grow their lovely lush green leaves
Autumn is when the temperature suddenly drops
The leaves change colour, then flutter gently to the ground
Winter is when it turns icy cold
It freezes, then snowflakes fall softly to the ground.

Jen Levy (10)
Knaphill Junior School, Woking

What's In The Box?

The orangy, red, fox
Runs around so happily,
There must be something in the box.

With its white, smooth tail
Blowing in the breeze,
The gentle tap against the box.

The gleaming eyes
It makes the face stand out,
It looks peaceful at the box.

Then something comes out
It's a small beautiful fox
So that was what was in the box.

Simon Gregory (11)
Knaphill Junior School, Woking

The Sea

I go up and down the sand
People always paddle in me
They walk up and down looking grand
Looking at everything they can see.

They hold their tasty ice cream
The grown-ups with their tea
Everyone is having fun it seems
What about me?

As I spray the young boys
When the wind is blowing it's fun
Pushing them about like cloth toys
I say to myself what's done is done.

Emma Spencer (11)
Knaphill Junior School, Woking

My Room

Mum screams 'Your room's a mess!'
OK, OK I will confess,
I dread the day though it will come,
When I hear this from Mum . . .
'Go and clean your room!'

Dad says 'You must clean up!'
I guess I'm being a mucky pup,
I quickly put it under my bed,
And the cupboard above my head
'Go and clean your room!'

Now that my room is clean,
No Mum or Dad being mean,
I can say to them 'Ha ha!
I don't have to clean my room!'

Louise Cobban (11)
Knaphill Junior School, Woking

Romans

R ed coated Romans
O n and on the army marched
M aybe a little too tough for the Celts
A strong army as well
N asty and tough
S trong as an ox.

Jack Duncan (8)
Knowepark Primary School, Selkirk

My Secret Garden

I've my own secret garden
Hidden in the bushes
There's only a tree stump to sit on,
It's full of different flowers
There's red and yellow
White and pink, they're as colourful as the rainbow
I love the tulips best,
When I go to smell the scent
They smell like Mum's perfume
And I can almost taste the honey sweetness.
They start off as seeds
Then grow into flowers
Their stems get longer
As their days get shorter
When I come from school
I rush into my secret garden
It fills me up with joy.

Rachael Keys (9)
Lack Primary School, Enniskillen

My Rabbit

My rabbit's name is Maisy
She likes to play with my brother's rabbit Daisy.
They skip and jump about the place
Sniffing everything with their little face.

They're black and white,
And their eyes are as brown as bears.
But the best of all was,
When we got them,
They were all cuddled up in a cardboard box,
As warm and cosy as a pair of woolly socks.

Kylie Noble (10)
Lack Primary School, Enniskillen

A Trip To The Zoo

People are singing,
Some phones are ringing,
Having lots of fun,
Playing in the sun.

People are delighted,
And some are excited,
On a big yellow bus as yellow as it can be,
For all of us to see.

People are sad,
Some are glad,
The tigers were roaring,
No rain was pouring.

The monkeys were skipping,
The birds were dipping,
One giraffe looked over,
And nearly ate me up.

We went to the shop,
It was filled up to the top,
When we got home it started to rain,
It was a very big pain.

Lorna Graham (10)
Lack Primary School, Enniskillen

Flowers!

Flowers are beautiful, bright and colourful,
Everywhere you go, flowers are always growing,
Their smell is as sweet as sugar and as fresh as day
You can pick them for your granny
Your mummy or your auntie
You can pick them for teacher
Or maybe even a friend
Put them in a pretty vase and fill it with some water.

Zana Bratton (9)
Lack Primary School, Enniskillen

Belfast Zoo

Everyone jumped onto the big bus,
We ran to a seat with a mighty fuss,
Everyone excited and over the moon,
We asked our teacher, 'Are we there soon?'
Lack, Ballygawley, M1,
Here we come
We arrive, and there are parrots squawking,
People talking,
Monkeys swaying,
Giraffes playing,
Lions growling,
Tigers prowling,
Zebras galloping everywhere.
Look! What's that? It is a bear!
Penguins waddling,
Seals doddling,
Then we had our lunch,
My juicy apple went munch, munch, munch,
I sulked in the bus, I was sad,
I fell asleep, my brother was glad.

Emma Forbes (10)
Lack Primary School, Enniskillen

Spurs FC

S is for the cool skills by Robbie Keane
P is for rough playing by Roy Keane
U is for the unwell footballer
R is for the red card that Robbie Fowler gets
S is for the shouting of the crowd

F is for the fantastic playing of Spurs
C is for lots of cheering when Spurs win.

Robert Corry (11)
Lack Primary School, Enniskillen

A Trip To The Zoo

As warm as tea was the day in summer,
Slowly but surely we got in lumber,
There was a jam in Belfast, that was new
You could not even hear a squeak on the view.

I saw a lion creeping closer and closer,
The tiger was dribbling and wanted some food.
Penguins waddling down the ice,
Seals playing like it was daylight.

Giraffes being as proud as peacocks
While zebras are being as scared as mice
Elephants running what a laugh,
The teachers drawing some lovely graphs.

Chimpanzees were lazy when we arrived,
Sleeping while visitors were passing by,
It was hilarious when the monkeys were dribbling,
Over the wall when my mum was eating.

Alison Neville (10)
Lack Primary School, Enniskillen

Belfast Zoo

B is for the big double decker bus taking us
E is for everything at the zoo like all the animals
L is for the very long journey up to Belfast
F is for the fast cheetah that runs around a lot
A is for all the animals at the zoo
S is for the snakes hissing
T is for the tiger prowling

Z is for the zebras' black and white stripes
O is for the outstanding performance of the monkeys
O is for all the other amazing animals at the zoo.

Emma Beacom (11)
Lack Primary School, Enniskillen

My Sister And I

I am mad as can be
With my sister on my knee
Full of temper and of hate
Why should I be bothered to eat
Furious, wicked as can be
With my head held on my knee
I stamp my feet 1, 2, 3
With my sister laughing
With glee
My face is as red
As a berry in a pot
I am just like a tot
Don't know what to do with
The jam pot
Open the lid and eat the lot
No I don't think this could be
Because I would be sick as can be
Hopefully tomorrow
I shall see the bright
Sun shining on me
Then I might realise
What happiness means
To me.

Jemma Walker (10)
Lack Primary School, Enniskillen

My Easter Holidays

E is for all the eggs I got
A is for all the fun we had
S is for all the sweets we had
T is for time of school we had
E is for Easter time when Jesus died
R is for when he rose again.

Julie Weir (9)
Lack Primary School, Enniskillen

I Love My Dad

I love all the cuddles
He gives to me
When I'm just sitting
On his cuddly knee.

He hugs me when
I need a big one
And my love for him is
Second to none.

My dad is as cuddly as
A little baby bunny
And when I really need it
He will give me money.

When I am out with him
He buys me sweets
And when I am at home with
Him he gives me treats.

He is the biggest
Bestest ever
I would never hurt
Him never! Never!

My dad buys me
Things for Christmas
And he says to me that
I am his little lass.

Gail Woods (10)
Lack Primary School, Enniskillen

The Wizard

In a castle, dark and gloomy
A wizard mixes magic spells . . .
Making potions in his fortress;
Some to drink and some to sell.

The sorcerer wears a pointed hat.
His cape is long and midnight blue.
His boots are tall with scarlet buckles,
Beards like his are very few!

His black cat sits by a glowing fire . . .
A shelf with special secret scrolls . . .
A watching raven on a roof beam . . .
Grey rats run to their hidden holes.

In his cauldron is a lizard
Mixed with dragons' scaly skin.
Newts and toads, and hairy spiders
Soon a princess will go in!

Here comes a knight with his banner flying
Over the wizard's drawbridge rides!
He draws his sword and with his crossbow
Shoots the wizard in the side!

The knight runs down to the warlock's dungeons
Splits with sword the door of stone . . .
Grips his weapon, breaks the shackles
Rescues the princess and takes her home!

Nathanael Brown (11)
Lack Primary School, Enniskillen

The Magic Socks

When I went to my friend's house
I found some magic socks,
I put them on and went to bed
And gave me quite a shock.
I flew into space, in the sky
Past the Milky Way
I suddenly stopped
Flew back down
And never flew back up, why?

Abigail Thompson-O'Connor
Leighfield Primary School, Uppingham

My Magic Socks

I have a pair of magic socks
They take me to the moon
It's as high as high
As a mountain in the sky.

I have a pair of magic socks
They make me want to run
When I'm playing with my friends
We have a lot of fun.

Charlotte Gregg (7)
Leighfield Primary School, Uppingham

This Is The Key To . . .

This is the key of the world
In that world is mud
In that mud is clay
In that clay is rock
In that rock is hot rock
In that hot rock is lava
In that lava are trapped creatures.

Edgar Ellis (8)
Leighfield Primary School, Uppingham

This Is The Key To . . .

This is the rusty key to the giant world
In the giant world is a cruel kingdom,
In that cruel kingdom is a dark wood,
In the dark wood there is a little lane,
At the end of the little lane is a large lake,
In the large lake is a sunken shipwreck,
In the sunken shipwreck is a rotten dining room,
In the rotten dining room is a large plate,
On the large plate is a crumbling skull,
In that skull was some rotten brains,
In those rotten brains is a hollow hall,
In the hollow hall is a load of white mice,
Next to the white mice is a load of brown mice,
They are dancing.

Molly Feely (9)
Leighfield Primary School, Uppingham

Daffodils

Daffodils look like ringing bells
Twinkling in the breeze.
Their stem as thin as a straw
Lots of petals in a circle
Their leaves as soft as velvet
Standing next to a little running river
Their reflection in the river.

Daffodils are beautiful shining in the rain
It is a shame that people pick them
Because they cannot grow again.
When they go they leave their petals where
They used to stand.

Grace Gutteridge (9)
Leighfield Primary School, Uppingham

Daffodils

Flying over the winter sky
Watching the daffodils grow
With the birds flying over me
As I watch the night-time snow.
As I fly over the sparkling sky
Over the mountains over the trees
I fly when I am singing a lullaby
My lullaby is about daffodils in the winter sky.

Henry Jones (9)
Leighfield Primary School, Uppingham

This Is The Key To . . .

On that earth there is a some land
On that land there is a country
In that country there is a city
In that city there is a town
In that town there is a crumbling village
In that crumbling village there is a house
In that house there is a cupboard
In that cupboard there is a biscuit.

Robert Fox (9)
Leighfield Primary School, Uppingham

This Is The Key To . . .

This is the key to the jungle
In that jungle there is a wood
In that wood there is a river
Down that river there is a waterfall
Down that waterfall there is a bamboo hut
In that hut there is a room
In that room there is a bamboo bed
And on that bed there is a red rose.

George Scott (9)
Leighfield Primary School, Uppingham

Animal Magnetism

I'm as attracted to you as
A builder to a brick,
I'm as attracted to you as
A footballer to a kick.

I'm as attracted to you as
A car to the road,
I'm as attracted to you as
A safe to a code.

I'm as attracted to you as
A chimney to a house,
I'm as attracted to you as
A cat to a mouse.

I'm as attracted to you as
A plane is to flying,
I'm as attracted to you as
A poet is to rhyming.

Luke Roberts (11)
Leighfield Primary School, Uppingham

This Is The Key To . . .

This is the key of the kingdom
In that kingdom there's a deep dark
wiggely wraggely path which the
bravest people go on,
Along the path is an abandoned street
They say the devils are having a party.
Down the street there is a haunted house.
In the house there is a cobweb filed staircase.
Up the stairs is a room and in the room
There is a bloodsucking vampire.

Hannah Rose (8)
Leighfield Primary School, Uppingham

Sonnet No 27

Shall I compare thee to a hairy mole?
Thy breath stinks as bad as a rotting pig,
Thy chest is as round as a kitchen bowl,
And that smelly mop on your head, a wig?

Thou est very similar to a horse,
Thy legs and knees are extremely knobbly,
Thou wouldst not complete an obstacle course,
Thy horrible, huge nose is wobbly.

Thy house is a dustbin on the main street,
Thy clothes have holes in them and smell like fish,
Thou have cheesy verrucas on thy feet,
And you think you've got a lover, you wish!

Thy make-up is like clowns', thou look a mess,
Can't you see I don't like you, did you guess?

Benjamin Kind & Joshua Wedge (11)
Leighfield Primary School, Uppingham

The Sea

The sea is a hungry shark
Giant and black
He rolls on the beach all day
With his wicked white teeth
And grey jaws
Biting at the people
All day long
The shark starts to feel sleepy
He slows down
His movements die down
Everything becomes calm.

Ryan Bennett (10)
Leighfield Primary School, Uppingham

The Moon

The moon is a friendly face smiling down
He has no voice
He has no hair
He only has a gentle stare.

The moon only sleeps
While the sun is out
And about.
He glides through the empty skies.

The moon is a great friend
His face is always cheerful;
He needs no voice to gladden me
Only the smile on his face.

Elizabeth Wignall (11)
Leighfield Primary School, Uppingham

This Is The Key To . . .

This is the key of the village
In that village there is a thin, small lane,
In that lane there is a tiny shop,
In that tiny shop there is a wooden counter,
Behind that wooden counter is a metal shelf,
On that metal shelf is a till,
Inside the till there is a ripped ten pound note,
On top of that ripped ten pound note
Is a shiny, glimmering coin,
On that coin is a newborn baby spider,
On that newborn baby spider is an old, mouldy breadcrumb.

Catherine Crook (9)
Leighfield Primary School, Uppingham

The Sea

The sea is a monstrous serpent,
Long and silver grey.
Slithering up upon the shore,
Hissing, screeching,
Digging his fangs into the sand,
The serpent clashes with the rocks,
Causing stones, stones, stones . . .
Tumbling stones to fall,
And when night is right,
Stormy clouds ahead,
The serpent rises up onto the cliffs,
Then screeches so loud
It can be heard from a huge distance,
Then on a quiet night in May or June,
It's time for him to leave.
He slowly lies on the wet sand,
So peaceful,
And rolls back across the sandy pebbles.

Georgia Huzar (11)
Leighfield Primary School, Uppingham

Daffodils

Daffodils are yellow and shiny,
Beautifully blonde,
Though they are so small and tiny,
You will find them by a sparkling pond.

Yellow like shimmering sun,
Stems whirling as they dance,
Their petals twirl as you run,
You can see the beauty in one glance.

Hurry 'cause they only stay
Until that very last spring day!

Phoebe Toms (9)
Leighfield Primary School, Uppingham

The Sea

The sea is a mad tiger,
Roaring and angry,
Spotting its prey,
Creeping closer and closer,
Then pouncing and crashing
. . . Its teeth sink in!

Roaring as if in pain,
He moans, groans, moans, groans,
Speeding as if in a race,
Then . . .
Splashing over the finish line!

When the skies go dark,
In May or June,
Calmer and calmer goes the sea,
Calmer and calmer goes the tiger,
And he sleeps under the starlit sky.

Georgina Mattock (11)
Leighfield Primary School, Uppingham

This Is The Key To . . .

This is the key to the city
In the city there is a tall building
In the tall building there is lots of rooms
In one of the rooms there is a bedroom
In that bedroom there is a door
Behind that door there is a bed
In that bed there is a child fast asleep.

Charlie Pallett (9)
Leighfield Primary School, Uppingham

The Sea

The sea is an elegant tabby cat,
She slouches on the beach all day and night
With her gentle lick and padded paws,
Hour upon hour she purrs,
Pouncing at the cliff.

But when the dark days come,
She is as angry as a lion,
Slashing at the rocks,
Shrieking and screeching,
She'll sink her teeth into you if you dare come near.

And on the calm days of May or June,
She ambles over rocks and pebbles,
If you come near,
She will only purr,
She will frolic with you,
In a playful way.

Laura Buzzard (11)
Leighfield Primary School, Uppingham

This Is The Key To . . .

This is the key to the city
In that city there is a lake full of ducks
Across that lake there is a field of sheep
Along the field there is a well
Down the well there is a tunnel full of darkness
Up and out of the tunnel there is a lane
Round the lane there is a house
Inside the house there is a bed
Under the covers there is a parcel
In the parcel there is a fresh flower.

Olivia Cowood (9)
Leighfield Primary School, Uppingham

I'm As Attracted To You As

I'm as attracted to you as
A bee is to making honey.

I'm as attracted to you as
A miser to saving money.

I'm as attracted to you as
A lion to meat.

I'm as attracted to you as
A dog to cheesy feet.

I'm as a attracted to you as
A boat to the water.

I'm as attracted to you as
Bricks to mortar.

I'm as attracted to you as
A ship to the sea.

I'm as attracted to you
As mud to a knee.

William Raynes (11)
Leighfield Primary School, Uppingham

Daffodils

Yellow as a lemon,
You flap in the breeze
Fine as a melon
You sing to the trees.

Trumpets blowing a single song,
You stand proud and fine,
Stems tall, green and strong,
I want you for one of mine.

Edward Wignall (9)
Leighfield Primary School, Uppingham

The Sea

The sea is a racing Japanese racer
With no regard for anything except itself
Racing, racing,
Clattering and shattering against water.
His sharp fangs rush against the seashore.
Soon he leaps above the sea line,
Louder! Louder! He calls until a massive tidal waves
Clashes down,
Under he goes.

Deeper, deeper to the seabed
Now he has settled like a rock
Down, down,
He goes.

Adam Willars (11)
Leighfield Primary School, Uppingham

Animal Magnetism

I'm as attracted to you as
A bee to making honey
I'm as attracted to you as a
Miser to saving money.

I'm as attracted to you as
A beetle to dung
I'm as attracted to you as
Air to the lung.

I'm as attracted to you as
A tourist to a map
I'm as attracted to you as
Eminem doing a rap.

Samuel Allen (10)
Leighfield Primary School, Uppingham

The Sea

The sea is a frolicking bear,
Baring his brilliant white teeth,
He rolls on the beach all day,
Prowling in and out of the waves,
Then dashing out towards the cliffs,
He growls and yowls under the dark night sky.

And in the symphony of the wind and the rain,
The giant sea-bear rages,
As if in pain,
As he bounds to his feet and plunges deep.

But in the quiet nights of May or June,
The sea-bear lying on the sandy shores,
Bows his head and yells no more.

Jessica Gray (11)
Leighfield Primary School, Uppingham

Socks

So many different types
Reds, greens and blues,
Spots, zigzags and stripes,
Which one do you choose?

Long socks, short socks,
Lots and lots to use,
Toe socks, no socks,
Which one do you choose?

So many to pick from
It will take forever
I can't choose just one
I'll have to wear them all together!

Laura Williams (11)
Leighfield Primary School, Uppingham

The Sea

The sea is a galloping horse
Big and dark,
Her mane flies up and down,
As she jumps out of the sand,
As the wind gets stronger,
She clashes against the cliffs,
And when the night wind roars,
And the moon rocks in the stormy clouds,
She gets to her feet and shakes her wet mane,
As she runs along the sand,
But on quiet days in May or June,
When even the grasses are still in the dune,
She lies on the sand,
So quiet, so quiet,
She scarcely moves.

Laura Wilks (10)
Leighfield Primary School, Uppingham

Volcano

The volcano is a furious giant
Belching up smoke at any second
His vicious hair sweeps across lands
People perish in his wake,
Leaving only cinders behind.
His temper rises as the day goes on,
His breath engulfs the air
And his red-hot hands slam down on the earth,
As the night goes on, his explosions speed
Through towns.
Finally,
When the dawn comes
He calms, until the dusk.

Kathryn Robinson (11)
Leighfield Primary School, Uppingham

The Sea

The sea is a galloping horse,
Lashing up onto the sand.
His mane flickers like white fire,
His hooves lashing around.
A long loud whine fills the air,
As he canters out of the bay
The moonlight shimmers around him,
His slender, smooth coat, his echoing bray.

The sea is a weary horse,
As day overwhelms night.
The dancing light around him,
Is sparkling, shining bright.
He lumbers onto the beach,
His tired legs collapse,
He settles down and calms himself,
He closes his eyes,
And naps.

Ruth Corbet (11)
Leighfield Primary School, Uppingham

Daffodils

D affodils are pretty
A nd very colourful too
F ading colours at the end of the day but
F unny when you watch then close up
O bviously beautiful in every way, and the
D affodils prance in the moonlight
I nside my house I watch them with glee!
L ovely things I think they are
S o smily, *I love daffodils!*

Hannah Gregg (9)
Leighfield Primary School, Uppingham

The Sea

The sea is wild horses, galloping along the beach,
Grey, playful and beautiful, rolling along the sand,
Rising up, up manes flowing in the breeze.

They dash and bash against the cliffs with a whip
From their tails,
They fling rocks from the cliffs.

And when night comes the wind roars
And the moon smiles at the shore from the stormy clouds,
Then they bound onto their hooves under the starlit sky.

But on quiet days of May or June,
They grow tired
And with a flick of their tails they're gone.

Jessica Torbell (11)
Leighfield Primary School, Uppingham

The Sea

The sea is a graceful tiger,
Ferocious and skilled,
He roars in the evening
And swallows up the sand.
He clatters his salty teeth
Against the jagged rocks
And brushes the shore with his silky fur.

Eventually he falls asleep
And his nocturnal dance is done
And the quiet days of May or June have begun.

Elliot Todd (11)
Leighfield Primary School, Uppingham

The Sea

The sea is a galloping horse,
Wild and free,
So graceful and gleeful,
Dashing its crystal clear wave,
Clashing and clanging,
Onto the shore.

Trotting on all day
Splashing its playmates
And swishing its tail
Splashing on the rocks,
Splash, splish, splosh.

He kicks in excitement,
And then gallops away,
Across the pebbly beach,
Clip, clop, clap.

Bethany Prior (10)
Leighfield Primary School, Uppingham

Tears

Tears of laughter
Tears of joy
Tears of sadness
Tears of a boy.

Tears help you recover
Tears help you smile
Tears of a mother
Tears of a crocodile.

Grace Hudson (10)
Leighfield Primary School, Uppingham

Animal Magnetism

I'm as attracted to you as a
Bee to making honey.
I'm as attracted to you as a
Miser to saving money.

I'm as attracted to you as a
Reporter is to the news,
I'm as attracted to you as
I am to a cruise.

I'm as attracted to you as
Ink is to a pen,
I'm as attracted to you as a
Cockerel to a hen.

I'm as attracted to you as a
Mouse is to cheese
I'm as attracted to you as
Pans are to peas.

Victoria Neill (11)
Leighfield Primary School, Uppingham

This Is The Key To . . .

This is the key to the city,
In that city there is a small village,
In that village there is a long road,
On that road there is a house,
In that house there is a titchy room,
In that room there is a snuggly bed,
On that bed there are stripy covers,
Under those covers is me!
Inside me are thoughts,
In those thoughts I am thinking
Gotta hide from my brother!

Hannah Ellwood (9)
Leighfield Primary School, Uppingham

Animal Magnetism

I'm as attracted to you as a mouse to cheese,
I'm as attracted to you as Holly to peas.

I'm as attracted to you as a bee to nectar,
I'm as attracted to you as a film to a director.

I'm as attracted to you as a bat to a cave,
I'm as attracted to you as a zombie to a grave.

I'm as attracted to you as a pig to food,
I'm as attracted to you as my sister to a mood.

I'm as attracted to you as Adam to Louise,
I'm as attracted to you as a door to keys.

I'm as attracted to you as a bounce to a ball,
I'm as attracted to you as a giraffe to being tall.

I'm as attracted to you as a sun to smiling
I'm as attracted to you as a phone to dialling.

Grace Sanders (11)
Leighfield Primary School, Uppingham

Animal Magnetism

I'm attracted to you as a cow to its moo,
I'm attracted to you as a foot to a shoe.

I'm attracted to you as a girl is shopping,
I'm attracted to you as a party popper is to popping.

I'm attracted to you as a cat is to purring,
I'm attracted to you as the wind is to whirling.

I'm attracted to you as a dictionary is to words,
I'm attracted to you as a whey is to curds.

I'm attracted to you as a tree is to soil,
I'm attracted to you as a kettle is to boil.

I'm attracted to you as a driver is to a car,
I'm attracted to you as a walker to going far.

Claire Garley (10)
Leighfield Primary School, Uppingham

Volcano

Exploding volcano,
Grumbling and growling.

        Bubbling lava,
        Sliding and gushing.

                Smoking volcano,
                Waving its sparkly red hair.

Lava sweeping out,
Running away.

        Volcano, grumbling out loud,
        Saying what it has to say.

                Lava. It's shiny eye glimmering
                Under the black steaming smoke.

Volcano, vomiting out flames,
Spitting out sparks.

        Lava, reaching out
        Its arm of fire.

                Volcano, like a firework,
                Smashing out its flames.

Bradley Toms (11)
Leighfield Primary School, Uppingham

Animal Magnetism

I'm as attracted to you as a bee to collecting pollen.
I'm as attracted to you as stars are to lighting the darkness.
I'm as attracted to you as teeth are to smiling.
I'm as attracted to you as crocodiles to living in a swamp.
I'm as attracted to you as cats are to catching mice.
I'm as attracted to you as a boy to watching telly.
I'm as attracted to you as a barn owl flying in the dark.
I'm as attracted to you as a tree to growing leaves.
I'm as attracted to you as a snowflake bringing the cold.

Louise Garley (10)
Leighfield Primary School, Uppingham

Animal Attraction

I'm as attracted to you as
A crocodile to snapping.
I'm as attracted to you as
Eminem to rapping.
I'm as attracted to you as
A boat to a river.
I'm as attracted to you as
A snake to its slither.
I'm as attracted to you as
A ninja to fighting.
I'm as attracted to you as
An electrician to lighting.
I'm as attracted to you as
A nit to hair.
I'm as attracted to you as
A dragon to its lair.
I'm as attracted to you as
A child to nag.
I'm as attracted to you as
A bully to brag.

Holly Montagnon (11)
Leighfield Primary School, Uppingham

Untitled

It stalks me by day
Waits to pounce by night
It was my one love
Now my one hate
My one scare
My one happiness
I hear it moaning, groaning, screeching,
The voice of the ghost.

Sian Evans (10)
Leighfield Primary School, Uppingham

Animal Magnetism

I'm as attracted to you as
A ghost is to scaring you
I'm as attracted to you as
A bug is to giving you flu.

I'm as attracted to you as
A soap is to cleaning
I'm as attracted to you as
A girl is to screaming.

I'm as attracted to you as
A spy is to spying
I'm as attracted to you as
A fly is to flying.
I'm as attracted to you as
A picture to a wall
I'm as attracted to you as
A footballer to a ball.

Samuel Evans (11)
Leighfield Primary School, Uppingham

The Magic Seed

Once I planted a magic seed
It grew into a monster
It wanted to eat me
It was big
It had red eyes
Gulp!
It ate me.

Jack De Wet (6)
Leighfield Primary School, Uppingham

I'm As Attracted To You As . . .

I'm as attracted to you
As bees to making honey.

    I'm as attracted to you as
    A miser to saving money.

I'm as attracted to you as
A boat to water.

    I'm as attracted to you as
    Bricks are to mortar.

I'm as attracted to you as
A foot to a ball.

    I'm as attracted to you as
    A shopper to a mall.

I'm as attracted to you as
A kangaroo to bouncing.

    I'm as attracted to you as
    Cats are to pouncing.

I'm as attracted to you as
Birds are to flying.

    I'm as attracted to you as
    Gollum to spying.

Isaac Parr (11)
Leighfield Primary School, Uppingham

Dad Likes Grand Prix

Dad likes Grand Prix
The drivers are dopey
The cars are red
After that
Dad goes to bed.

Douglas J Douglas (6)
Leighfield Primary School, Uppingham

The Sea

The sea is a nervous cat
Leaping with endless energy
Constantly bounding onto the beach
Spitting at the cliffs
Scraping at the rocks
Hour upon hour she bites
The rumbling, tumbling stones
And groans, groans, groans, groans
The ocean cat moans
Licking the sour sea salt
And when the night wind roars
And the moon rocks in the blustery clouds
She climbs up the cliffs
Sticking her paws deep into the rocks
Still spitting at the sand
And screeching and squealing
Loud and bold
But on her silent days
She gracefully rolls up the beach
Wading and curling through the sand
And gently breathes.

Tilly Jones (11)
Leighfield Primary School, Uppingham

I Planted Some Seeds

I bought some seeds
I planted one of them
I told it what to do first.

Grow some roots
Then you must grow a stem.

Then some leaves
Then a flower.

Francis Wignall (5)
Leighfield Primary School, Uppingham

My Shadow Friend

She sits there with me
On a summer's day
We talk, walk and skip.

I go to the park
And play with her,
But the see-saw never tips.

My daddy puts me
In my swing
And her daddy puts her in hers.

We both get pushed
At the same time
But her swing never creaks or whirls.

We go round on a
Roundabout,
I will go fast; it may, it might.
And if our daddies
Spin us quick
We will have to hold on tight!

Rachelle Bartlett (11)
Leighfield Primary School, Uppingham

Flowers

Flowers can grow
Flowers are big
Flowers are lovely
Flowers are good
I love flowers.

Rebecca Wootton (5)
Leighfield Primary School, Uppingham

Tractors

I went to a tractor shop
I got an 8420
It was the biggest of the Richard John Deers
It had active seats
It had an eighteen speed triptronic.
Fully automated gear box

It can hold any man in comfort
Twelve hours a day
Day in and day out
And still feeling very comfortable.

Hector Thorne (6)
Leighfield Primary School, Uppingham

The Ferrari

One day I drove a Ferrari
It went ninety miles an hour
There was a sharp corner
I skidded
A tractor was going into the field
I crashed and the pick-up truck
Had to get me out.

James Flavell (6)
Leighfield Primary School, Uppingham

A Seed

I planted a seed
The seed fell in the weed.
It fell near the wall.
It grew very tall.

Adam Roberts (6)
Leighfield Primary School, Uppingham

My Year

January brings snowy skies,
Sip hot chocolate by the fire.
February brings ice and frost,
Snowdrops peep and have a look.
March brings lambs that prance about,
Daffodils begin to sprout.
April brings showers of rain and flowers,
Scatters daisies at our feet.
May brings a pretty pole,
Entwined with ribbons top to toe.
June brings my birthday treat,
Lots of fun and things to eat.
July brings sports day (sunny we hope)
Come on Oak, Come on Oak!
August brings the hot holidays,
Au revoir l'anglettere, a bien tôt.
September already? Back to school,
New class, new teacher, but old friends.
October brings autumn colour,
Reds, oranges, yellows and gold.
November brings Guy Fawkes' night,
Bonfires, sparklers, rockets bright.
December brings Christmas time,
Pull some crackers have some wine!
Which of these do you like best?
This is not a trick or test.
It's too difficult to decide,
When each month is so divine.
If I really have to say,
I just love every single day.

Tessa Cooper (7)
Leighfield Primary School, Uppingham

Oliver's Poem

Dandelions are yellow
Grass is green
Trees are big
Pumpkins are orange
Stinging nettles are bad.

Oliver Dean (5)
Leighfield Primary School, Uppingham

Magic Mice

I love the magic mice in the kettle
And the magic mice can take me to the moon
And to see the stars
We go to Mars
And then I eat chocolate bars.

Robert Johnson (7)
Leighfield Primary School, Uppingham

The Fence

I help my dad to fix the fence
To make the garden tidy
My mum brings the tea to the workers
We all have a rest.

Jack Morris (6)
Leighfield Primary School, Uppingham

Spring

In the garden the sun is shining
The blossom is on the trees
It is spring.

Melissa Willars (5)
Leighfield Primary School, Uppingham

The Weird House

There once was a house and in that house
There was a mat and on the mat was a hat.
The cat chased the rat, and the rat chased the bat.
The bat had a cap, the cap fell in the hat.
The bat fell in the hat.
The rat got in and the cat got in the hat,
And the cat hopped on to the mat
The bat got the cap out.
The same with the cat and the rat.

Amy Hunting (7)
Leighfield Primary School, Uppingham

Magic Hat

My hat is no ordinary hat
It's a magic hat
And takes me anywhere I want
It's a magic hat
It helps me with my homework.
I went to London and halfway back
I went around the London Eye.

Harry Hathaway (7)
Leighfield Primary School, Uppingham

Poem Ideas

Magic shoes, magic shoes, take me into space
So I can see the planets.
Magic shoes, magic shoes, take me underground
So I can see the worms.

William Johnson (7)
Leighfield Primary School, Uppingham

The Magic Pet

My pet rabbit is black
A pitch-black little thing
His name is Spark
He glows in the dark
Whenever I say to him 'Take me somewhere!'
He will take me out to space,
Either to Mars or Pluto.
On Mars I eat chocolate bars
On Pluto I find aliens in the craters.
I tried to make him take me to Saturn!
But he won't.
My rabbit is so annoying sometimes.

Lewis Jennings (7)
Leighfield Primary School, Uppingham

A Tiger Came To Tea One Night

A tiger came to tea one night
'Who invited him?' I asked.
The room looked very small to me
It looked very tight.
I offered him a sandwich, but he ate the lot
I offered him a drink as he was very hot.
A tiger came to tea one night and ate the garden shed.

Beatrix Wignall (7)
Leighfield Primary School, Uppingham

My Magic Pet

My magic pet takes me to weird places
My magic pet is a kitten that does knitting
And makes me a woolly jam jumper.
I have it every day, but instead making it with wool
She makes it with raspberry jam.

Megan Wright (7)
Leighfield Primary School, Uppingham

Terrific Train

Terrific train drives in the rain
It starts up its engine
Then it arrives
And then we wave bye.
It drives away quickly to pick up the others
Then it goes past lots of mothers.
He goes away, he drives away,
He does that every single day.

Calypso Keightley (7)
Leighfield Primary School, Uppingham

The Magic Glasses

I love my magic glasses
They take me everywhere
And when I am in the street, everyone will stare.

I love my magic glasses
They take me to the moon
And when I'm on the moon, I'll sail away in a balloon.

Emogene Bromwich (7)
Leighfield Primary School, Uppingham

Magic Glasses

I love my magic glasses, they take me to the moon.
I just love my magic glasses, they make a funny tune.
I just love my magic glasses, they take me up in a balloon.
I have to go back home now, my tea is very soon.

Hollie Denney (7)
Leighfield Primary School, Uppingham

The State Of Art

Colours are spilling, melting and squirting,
Like the beautiful rainbow crashing through the sky.
Images are formed on the wall as a pencil mark
scrapes the wonderful sketches and designs.
The brush moves,
Like the wind blowing and writhing through the air
As the sun starts to set,
Like the sea splashing and whirling round and round
In a circle.
The colours blend to create new shades.
He takes a step back and admires his new picture
As if he were a loving mother to a child.
He sways his brush for the final touches to make
His picture perfect.

Leighton Davies (11)
Moorland Primary School, Cardiff

My Favourite Thing

I like cats all furry and white,
And I like the wind so I can fly a kite.
I like going to the beach,
And me and my brother having an ice cream each.
I like teddies all soft and hairy,
My favourite names are Abigail and Mary.
I like going on long journeys,
I like opening doors with keys.
My favourite pop group is S Club 8
And I like swinging on a gate.

So that is the end of my poem
If you have friends go and show 'em!

Charlotte Hogg (8)
Mundford Primary School, Thetford

The Clumsy Angel

There was a clumsy angel
She lived on a very dark strange hill
She didn't have any friends
The evil angel had all the best trends
But clumsy angel only had a tatty dress
Out of them all she wasn't the best
There was a job to do
It was to find a tiger for a zoo.

All the angels crowded around the boss
The angels were worried and a bit cross
At last he decided it was Charlie's Angels
Nobody was really surprised, nobody opened their eyes
The clumsy angel decided to spy on them
She stepped on a loose hem.

They caught the tiger all together
Now they are friends and they shall stay forever
They put the tiger back in the zoo
Charlie's Angels said 'Here's a present for you.'

Hannah Dolman (9)
Mundford Primary School, Thetford

The Bowling Alley Blues

The spirit is high
Hear the tune, super.
Every time they hit a strike
They're heroes
Bowling leg ends and heroes cheer
So as old as the bowling alley may be with crumbling frames
It is still in service.

Christopher Walkey (9)
Mundford Primary School, Thetford

Me And Hannah

My best friend is Hannah
I call her Spanna
For a nickname
She is good at games.

Hannah likes gymnastics
She's good on the floor
But sometimes she hits the door
Which is a tiny bit poor
But she still does some more.

We do gymnastics for PE
But me and Hannah hurt our knee.

I can't do a handstand
If I have a hair band
Nor a roly-poly.

Me and Hannah go to ballet
We go on Tuesday
In Stoke Ferry
But I used to go to Bury.

Sophie Boulton (8)
Mundford Primary School, Thetford

My Great Cat

Once upon a time,
I have to make an excellent rhyme,
I have a ginger fabulous cat
Who always lays on the comfy, furry mat.
He is very sleepy and lazy,
And he is so very mental and crazy.
He likes to sleep snuggled and curled up
And he likes to drink from his special cat cup,
However he is excellent and clever
He has lots of friends always and will forever.

Megan Wharf (8)
Mundford Primary School, Thetford

Spring Fields

There are fields all around you
What do you want to do?
Do you want to play in the swishy grass,
Or maybe even pass?

There are fields all around you
Ah choo!
Excuse me
But I'm eating a pea
Well I'm sorry.

There are trees all around me
Slurp
I'm drinking my tea
Do you think it was me?

There are trees all around me
Hey I think I can see the sea
Do you want to swim with me?

There is ocean all around us
I'm just going to book a bus
Be quiet back there, stop all the fuss.

James Elwood (8)
Mundford Primary School, Thetford

Crazy Cat

My cat jumped on the window
He fell and hit the floor
He made himself a coffee
And then spilt it all over the door.
Brand new all white,
Now all brown and smells terrible,
It's only just been painted
Mum and Dad will think *bad*.

Halima Khan (8)
Mundford Primary School, Thetford

Monsters

In my house I am quite alone
All I can hear are the monsters' groans.

I'm not scared, well I am a bit
Oh no! The candle's lit.

I see monster shadows on the wall
But I know it's only my dog in the hall.

Argh! The dog's barking I'm not alone
Oh no! Someone else is in my home.

Oh no! I'm not alone!
Help! Help!

Oh, it's only Mum
The lottery she must have won!

Now I'm never alone
Yes, yes Mum's at home.

Ashlie White (8)
Mundford Primary School, Thetford

Space Dog And Me

There was an old dog from space
Who had a very ugly face.
His favourite food was rotten peas
And he sometimes nibbled his knees.
He lived on planet Mars
Back then there was no such thing as cars.
His favourite game was ball
He sometimes worked at a stall.
I guess he just isn't my type of dog,
I know, I'll get a frog.

Daniel Nicholls (10)
Mundford Primary School, Thetford

A Springer Dog

There once lived a springer dog
That always played around in the fog
It made him laugh
And everyone thought he was daft.

There once lived a springer dog
He liked to play around every day
He smelt a daisy and it went up his nose
And all the way down to his toes.

He likes to drive
Of course he's alive
He likes to sleep
And wake up and leap.

Darryl Wilson (10)
Mundford Primary School, Thetford

Busted

Busted are so cool
I met them once in a swimming pool
They said 'Hi dude' to me
Matt dived out of a tree
James made me jump
Charlie fell over with a bump
Let's have a swimming race
James was swimming at such a pace.
James said 'I won, I won,'
'Let's have a party under the sun.'
'Goodbye, goodbye, we have to go
We hope you'll come and watch our show.'

Leona Stubbings (8)
Mundford Primary School, Thetford

Weather

I don't know whether the weather is cold or hot
I can't believe I forgot
I don't know whether the weather is rain or snow,
I think my mum will know.

It's going to rain
No! It's going to hail
As a weatherman I think I'll fail.

I don't know whether the weather is hail or fog
I bought a cat and called him Mog.

Carl Brooks (10)
Mundford Primary School, Thetford

Tornado

Destruction, mayhem,
Twirling, churning,
Spinning violently,
Thrashing
Lure him, lunging
This evil monster
Stops at nothing.

Tony Way (10)
Mundford Primary School, Thetford

Young Man

There was a young man called Harry
Who lived with his cousin called Barry
It was a schoolday
So they went out to play
With the snow and made a snowman called Larry.

Jake Patrick (10)
Mundford Primary School, Thetford

What's The Best?

Christmas or my woolly vest?

Christmas is cool
It's the best
I don't know what's better
Christmas or my woolly vest?

My vest is warm
And cuddly too.

I just don't know what is the best
I've made my mind up, my woolly vest.

Fern Stannett (9)
Mundford Primary School, Thetford

Cinderella

I can't believe I've missed it all,
I've missed a chance to go to the ball.
I wonder if there's Gareth Gates,
He'd be dancing with his mates.
But anyway he probably stinks,
Or he could be on a date with Pink.
Fairy Godmother hear my call,
Could you take me to the ball?
In fancy shoes and a miniskirt,
Or maybe a top that says *alert!*
Ping, pang pong and a little song,
I'm at the ball in no time at all.
But now it's over it was just a dream,
I do not know how it could seem,
Like it weren't a lovely dream.
I can't tell you more,
My mouth is sore.
Bye for now,
I have to go and milk the cow.

Rebecca Brown (9)
Old Warren Primary School, Lisburn

Cindy

Cindy shouted and started to scream,
'Please let me go you're being so mean,
It's not fair, I want to go,
Everytime I ask, you always say no!'

So that was it she had made up her mind,
So now her clothes she had to find.
As she called her friend on her mobile phone,
She decided that she would no longer moan.
She put on her skirt, her make-up and shoes,
While her friend went to get some booze.

Tonight's the night she would find her fella,
From now on no sleeping in the cellar.
She heard the horn and jumped into the cab,
'When my sisters see me they will say I look fab.'

She got to the dance and everyone stared.
Her sisters made fun but she knew that they cared
The bloke who stood up was a good looking man,
He owned a countryside of land.
They kissed and danced and left together,
And their love for each other lasted forever.

Kayleigh Laybourn-Houston (10)
Old Warren Primary School, Lisburn

Moonlight

Craters, holes, deep, big and fat,
Asteroids, flying ships crossing the moon,
Silver moon glowing through space,
Yellow beams in the sky,
Shiny waters and windows in the sky.

Neal Archer (7)
Old Warren Primary School, Lisburn

Cinderella

All the time I didn't know
I'm not to go to the big disco.
I know I'll have one of my own
I will invite the prince you know.
We'll dance all night and all day
We might get married in sunny May.
My sisters will cry and be very sad
If my Prince Charming sets the day.

Hurry Godmother, hurry up
I have to go to the disco non-stop.
In time my dear I'm going fast
The disco doesn't start until half-past
You have until the clock strikes midnight
Then you will be in such a fright.
Old things you'll have, jeans and a top
And back home you will have to hop.
Good luck and don't get in a flop.

At the disco the lights were bright
And I looked like a shining light
In my miniskirt and glittering top
I saw the prince and he looked hot.
We danced and jived in the bright lights
Until the clock struck midnight
The spell was broken with the prince's kiss
And we were in heavenly bliss.

Kirsty Gorman
Old Warren Primary School, Lisburn

Food

Chips golden as treasure,
Bananas yellow as The Simpsons,
Meat brown as a bear,
Blackberries black as night.

Samuel Dowds (8)
Old Warren Primary School, Lisburn

Cheese

Cheese yellow as a pencil,
Cheese yellow as bananas,
Cheese yellow as my football,
Cheese yellow as sunshine,
Cheese yellow as a flower!

Glenn McCutcheon (8)
Old Warren Primary School, Lisburn

The Crazy Giant

My age is one hundred and sixty two
And I sound like a croaking frog
I think I was in the clouds over the zoo
And I am now in a misty fog.

Adam Collins (7)
Poringland Primary School, Poringland

The Giant With Sharp Teeth

My age is two hundred and forty six
And my teeth are extremely sharp
This is because I eat lots of chicks
And my teeth got stuck in a harp.

Gareth Phipps (8)
Poringland Primary School, Poringland

The Giant With Sharp Teeth

My age is one hundred and sixty six
And my teeth are as sharp as can be,
I went to the dentist to get them fixed,
And he said, 'Don't drink any more tea!'

William Warnes (7)
Poringland Primary School, Poringland

Spring

Spring comes around
Once every year,
You look at the ground
It's a pretty sight to see,
Trees and flowers,
Begin to bud,
While all the bees
Begin to buzz.

The birds bring
A lovely tune to sing
Then they go
To find a place to rest
So they go,
To make a nest.

Zoe Curtis (11)
Premnay School, Insch

Haiku

Shivering icebergs
Silvery, misty, turquoise
Indigo and blue.

Emma Sim (9)
Premnay School, Insch

Without You

Without you I am like
A star with no twinkle.
I'm like a moon without stars
Or a heart that doesn't beat.
Without you I'm like
A sea that is dry.

Without you I'm like
A bird that can't fly.
Without you I'm like
A house with no roof,
Or a sky with no flies.

Without you I'm like
A squirrel that can't climb.
Without you I'm like
A lost child in the jungle.
For, whatever I do you always
Understand me.

Rachael Feely (8)
St Eugene's Primary School, Knocks

How Strange

How strange to think that someone else
Lived in this house before
That someone had used my cupboards
And played on my floor.

Was it a man, a woman, a girl or a boy?
I'm confused and curious.

I wonder if they're still alive?
When I'm gone they'll share my home
With someone they love.

Sarah McGoldrick (9)
St Eugene's Primary School, Knocks

My Magic Box
(Based on 'Magic Box' by Kit Wright)

I will put in my box
A picture of me and my class
The cuddly toys I have
My first dog
And a big juicy Mars bar.

I will put in my box
A picture of me and my family
The biggest pizza in the world
My very sad tear
My first baby book.

I will put in my box
My first fluffy yellow chick
My family who have died
And a picture of my school.

Lisa Ingram (9)
St Eugene's Primary School, Knocks

I Will Put In My Box
(Based on 'Magic Box' by Kit Wright)

I will put in my box
My nice warm, comfy, soft, fluffy bed.
My parents' love and joy.
My first football that I got from Santa.
My PlayStation so that I can play all my
Favourite games on it.

I will put in my box
A big bulldog bigger than an Alsation.
My favourite kind of food with red sauce all over it.
My first trip to Spain on a hot summer's day
My big, black quad that is faster than the wind.

Ryan Carney (7)
St Eugene's Primary School, Knocks

My Magic Box
(Based on 'Magic Box' by Kit Wright)

I will put in my magic box
My favourite dog that hunts really well
Which is brown and white.

I will put in my magic box
All my friends that make me laugh more
Than ever
All the people in Heaven who have died.

I will put in my magic box
The first ball I kicked that was black and white
A bright sun that never goes out - not even at night
The biggest dinner ever I ate in my life.

My box has four leather corners
The top of the lid has a sun
On each side is a picture of Henrik Larsson.

Colin Logan (9)
St Eugene's Primary School, Knocks

The Grandfather Clock

There's a grandfather clock in my house,
It goes
Ding dong! Bing bong!
All day long.

I can't get to sleep at night-time
When it goes,
Ding dong! Bing bong!
All night long,
And it goes
Tick-tock! Tick-tock!
Oh! that big grandfather clock,
Big, long and tall
It stands in a corner.

Aoife Maguire (8)
St Eugene's Primary School, Knocks

My Magic Box
(Based on 'Magic Box' by Kit Wright)

I will put in my box
My fluffy pink piglet teddy bear,
My cushion that says fairy girl on it,
Some of my cat hairs.
My secrets book and my necklace.

I will put in my box
The ball that my auntie got me, it is bright, bright, bright pink
A stick my sister's dog chewed on. You can see his teethmark in it.
My ring that I got from Malta, just sparkling in the sun
My Winnie the Pooh jewellery box, hear the music that it plays.
The biggest shiniest star ever in the world.

My box is bright purple.
On the sides are pink roses.
The lid is made of seashells, wee baby ones like clams.
The corners are made with pips from a Granny Smith apple.
The bottom of it is made out of pink clay.

Eimir Maguire (8)
St Eugene's Primary School, Knocks

How Strange

How strange to think that someone else,
Lived in this house before,
Did they mess their room?
Or did they keep it tidy?

Were they polite?
Or were they rude?
All these questions to ask,
What was their favourite room?
What games did they play?

Will someone think of me when I'm gone?
I know that this is the best house ever.

Mark O'Reilly (9)
St Eugene's Primary School, Knocks

In The Summer

In the summer I like to play
At the beach, I'd like to go there today
But I would love if I was the
Only one on it.
I could be the first in line for ice cream
But sometimes I like people
If I was the only one there I'd be lonely,
I love the beach in the summer
The people playing volleyball
And the boys on quads.

In Winter
In winter the beach isn't crowded
No ice cream
Just people that didn't care
Left their rubbish lying there.
The waves crashing against the rocks
And the water turning black
The crabs swimming away and so are the fish
The lonely beach in winter
Oh I hate the beach in winter.

Raymond Logan (10)
St Eugene's Primary School, Knocks

My Microwave

My microwave it is like a cow
It is always mooing.
It's on a constant spin,
The noise it makes.
Bizzing, whirring, pinging
It drives me up the wall.
It is the most terrible noise
Its banging you could hear it a mile away.
When the bell rings, what a relief!
But oh there's one more twist.
The door - it's a tumbling disaster.

Cathal O'Neill (9)
St Eugene's Primary School, Knocks

Summer

All the people crazy
And some are so relaxed
The sun is gleaming down
Young children running around
Some people making sandcastles
Others are putting on their sunglasses
Children have suncream on
They're laughing as they throw the ball
In the water people are swimming round
Others have ice cream to cool them down
It's a pity it's not summer every day
If it were I'd be here to stay!

Winter
The beach so quiet
The air so cold
If you went now you'd be all alone
The sea is a blackly blue
There might be a windsurfer or two
You could walk a dog
If there's not a fog.

Sinead Rice (10)
St Eugene's Primary School, Knocks

Did You See?

Did you see the beautiful colours,
Sparkling in the jet-black sky?
Did you hear the screech,
As they were set off?
Did you smell the jacket potatoes,
With the toppings of corned beef and cheese?
Did you feel the cold night,
Nipping your cheeks and nose?
Did you taste the crunch,
From the chocolate apple?

Joely Emms (9)
St Joseph's Catholic Primary School, Wesham

My Alien

My alien has gold skin,
That can stick to walls.

My alien has eyes that have X-ray vision,
So beware in the shower.

He has a pod that flies,
He takes me to school in it.

My alien eats plasma . . . it's all gory.
And he sicks it out again, making me ill.

He has two arms that can stretch
Up to forty-eight metres . . . that's longer than ten cars.

He has one hundred razor-sharp teeth
That can cut through metal like butter.

His name is Rajack.
I call him this because Mum wouldn't let me call my dog Rajack!

Thomas Thain (7)
St Joseph's Catholic Primary School, Wesham

One Orange Ocelot

One orange ocelot ate an orange onion.
Two tiny tigers tiptoed to the street.
Three thinking therapists thatched a theatre.
Four fierce fighting ferrets flew to fairyland.
Five falling, flitting feathers, shouted 'Feather us.'
Six sacks of spuds sported spikes.
Seven sliding slugs slid silently, very slowly.
Eight eating elephants ate everything.
Nine naughty hair nits snatched a knot of neighbouring nits.
Ten twinkling tortoises trotted through tall trees.

Laura Hall (8)
St Joseph's Catholic Primary School, Wesham

Ten Things About My Alien

My alien has orange hair,
That trails out behind it.

My alien has white skin,
So he blends in with the front door.

He can twist his head a full turn.
Now that's a gift and a half.

His skin's like a basketball,
So I don't let him in my bed.

When my alien's in danger,
It runs up the wall.

He eats fish heads
And he won't eat anything else.

He likes to sit on the couch and watch TV
Just like me.

It just has one head,
With one eye to see through.

He likes playing with my cards,
So I have to shoo him off.

I think my alien . . .
Is the best!

Bradley Johnson (9)
St Joseph's Catholic Primary School, Wesham

My Alien

My alien has blue hair,
That goes to his kneecaps.

My alien has six heads,
Each with three eyes on.

My alien walks on the ceiling,
Instead of the floor.

My alien bumps
Into everything.

Joseph Clarke (8)
St Joseph's Catholic Primary School, Wesham

Mummy What Was A Gorilla?

Each ear was turned to the squawking of the parakeet,
Each face was bruised to the eye,
Each fist was weak,
Unchanged since time began.

Each body was strong and grand,
And each new baby creature is born
Another dawn will break
With the cry of a great beast, trying to live.

Now the darkness will spread so far,
Once a blossoming jungle,
Man could have helped this poor creature
But no, they didn't at all.
This creature's face was beaming
Clambering over the plants;
They didn't know the day would come
When they were left to die.

Before we were silenced
Hear our song,
Before we were silenced,
Hear our cry.

Olivia Wylde (10)
St Stephen's CE Junior School, Twickenham

The Hare And The Tortoise

A hare showed off to a tortoise one day,
'You're a great deal slower than me!'
The tortoise was tired of the boasting hare,
And said, 'I disagree!'

The hare was rather angry,
He ordered a race,
The tortoise was unsure
Until he remembered his steady pace!

The day of the race soon came,
Everyone was ready,
The hedgehog blew his gun
Then the tortoise went on steady!

The hare started very fast,
Then decided to have a snooze,
He dreamt of the finish line,
Not knowing his sleep would make him lose.

The tortoise passed the sleeping hare,
At his steady pace,
Very, very, very, soon
He would win the silly race.

The tortoise plodded on
The race was nearly done,
Before the hare knew,
The silly race was won!

Molly Riglin (9)
St Stephen's CE Junior School, Twickenham

Anger

Anger is like red-hot fire
It tastes like rotten blue cheese
It looks very damp
It feels very bad inside.

Ben Winward (7)
St Stephen's CE Junior School, Twickenham

Fireworks

F ireworks are very bright
I am scared
R oasted guy on the fire
E xcitement in the sky, that's fireworks
W hoosh, Boom! Bang!
O ooh look at that one
R eally high in the sky
K or! Wow look at that one
S uper, I love fireworks.

Lottie Fogg (7)
St Stephen's CE Junior School, Twickenham

Spider, Spider

Spiders, spiders are so scary
Spiders, spiders are so hairy
Spiders, spiders in the bath
Spiders, spiders make me laugh
Spiders, spiders in the sink
Spiders, spiders I need a drink!
Spiders, spiders on the light
Spiders, spiders get a terrible fright!

Billy Cohen (8)
St Stephen's CE Junior School, Twickenham

Black

Black is like the night
Creeping forward
It tastes like cold blood
It smells like dead bats and cats
It looks like a dead wood
Out there it sounds like wolves crying.

Caitlin Blyth (8)
St Stephen's CE Junior School, Twickenham

Happiness

Happiness is like the sun!
Happiness is yellow like bananas!
Happiness tastes like chocolate! Yummy!
Happiness smells like Christmas tea!
Happiness looks like flowers in a field!
Happiness sounds like fun!
Happiness feels like a nice furry coat!
That's what happiness really is!

Alexandria Gutman (7)
St Stephen's CE Junior School, Twickenham

Spider

Spider, spider make me wink
Spider, spider make me drink
Spider, spider make me blink
Spider, spider make me stink
Spider, spider make me sink
Spider, spider make me pink
Spider, spider make me think.

Hebe Naylor (7)
St Stephen's CE Junior School, Twickenham

The Sun Is

The sun is shining on the land
The sun is burning
The sun is flaming
The sun is fizzling
The sun is fire
The sun is . . .

William Jenkins (7)
St Stephen's CE Junior School, Twickenham

Excitement

The colour of excitement is bright yellow like the sun,
The feel of excitement is jolly and fun,
The sound of excitement is laughter and chat,
The smell of excitement is sweets and cakes
The look of excitement is bright and shiny,
The taste of excitement is juicy and sweet.

Lucy Theobald (8)
St Stephen's CE Junior School, Twickenham

Waves

The waves splashing against the rocks,
Giant waves hitting the shore,
The wind and the stars above,
Thunder striking the land and the sea,
Now the sun has come to brighten things up,
Now the people have come to fix things up.

Matthew Parsons (7)
St Stephen's CE Junior School, Twickenham

The Ocean

Big, big waves clashing against bare rocks
A cross and angry sea forcefully spreading
Huge drops go sinking down, down,
The sea leads out to a wide ocean
And that's the end of that!

Madeline Ralph (7)
St Stephen's CE Junior School, Twickenham

Fireworks

Bing bang everything is quiet until
   Sparkle
   Glitter
  Everything is wonderful
  When I am in bed
  Finally it is quiet
    But
      No
        I
          Cannot
        Go
      To
    Bed
      There
        Is
          Still
            More
  Exciting things to do.

Carys Thomson (7)
St Stephen's CE Junior School, Twickenham

Fear

It tastes like cold food!
It looks like a black sky!
It smells like red raw blood!
Its colour is black!
It sounds like the roar of a lion!
It feels like being inside a clam!

Megan Jones (7)
St Stephen's CE Junior School, Twickenham

Excitement

The colour of excitement is shiny gold
The taste of excitement is red-hot chilli
Excitement smells like a ripe juicy orange
Excitement looks like a huge wave
Excitement sounds like bells tingling
Excitement feels like red flames mixing inside you.

Phoebe Tupper (7)
St Stephen's CE Junior School, Twickenham

Happiness

Happiness is a colourful bright yellow sun
It tastes like happiness flowing all around me
It smells like fish and chips
It looks like a big smile on my face
It sounds like crisp crunching
It feels like bright lipstick.

Kaja Redler (7)
St Stephen's CE Junior School, Twickenham

Sleepy

It is pink like blossom
It tastes like marshmallows
It smells like red roses
It looks like wild flowers
It sounds like birds singing
It feels like a lazy day.

Lucy Whitear (8)
St Stephen's CE Junior School, Twickenham

Happiness

Happiness is like the colour yellow
Like the yellow sun
It tastes like Christmas pudding
It smells like a red rose
It looks like a field of flowers
It sounds like birds cheeping
It feels like a soft cover.

Emma Davies (8)
St Stephen's CE Junior School, Twickenham

Happiness

Happiness is like the red hot sun
It tastes like chips in a hot bowl
It smells like roses in a flower bed
It looks like a new car
It sounds like raindrops falling onto your house
It feels like jumping into a swimming pool.

Thomas Drew (7)
St Stephen's CE Junior School, Twickenham

Anger

Anger looks like a ripe tomato!
Anger tastes like a red hot pepper!
Anger feels like lightning has just struck
Anger smells like yellow hot fires
Anger sounds like a mega boulder is *coming*.

Matthew Fletcher (8)
St Stephen's CE Junior School, Twickenham

The Writer Of This Poem
(Based on 'The Writer Of This Poem' by Roger McGough)

The writer of this poem is as silly as a mouse
He is as small as a spec
As stretchy as Blu-tack
As stupid as a tree.

As fast as the speed of light
As wise as the three kings
As shiny as gold
As light as thin air.

As mean as a pirate
As slim as a fish
As big as the Atlantic Ocean.

The writer of this poem
Never ceases to amuse
He's one in a million billion
(Or the poem says).

Henry Day (8)
St Stephen's CE Junior School, Twickenham

A Pupil's Prayer

Let the teachers all be kind
Never let it cross their mind
That maybe I will get a warning
The very first thing in the morning.
Please let them give me the very best
Especially in spelling tests.
Let the school dinners all be nice
And not be horrid meat and rice.
Oh please let games on the pitch
Not be cuts and scabs you want to itch.
Please let children not tease me
Because I'm rubbish at literacy.

Ruby Woolfe (9)
St Stephen's CE Junior School, Twickenham

I Miss You

The sky is high
But not as high as Heaven
I watched you go slowly as you went away
With tears coming down my face I would like to say
'I love you and I'll love you forever.'
It's not the same not having you by my side.
I'm lonely not having you here
But I promise I'll see you soon.

Eleanor McKone (7)
St Stephen's CE Junior School, Twickenham

My Box
(Based on 'Magic Box' by Kit Wright)

I will put in my box
The smell of petals
The smell of the sea
The sight of the money growing tree.

I will put in my box
The sound of birds whistling in the morning
The sound of rocks crashing together
The sound of a baby laughing.

I will put into the box
The sight of a fierce tiger
The feel of my hair when it's been cut
The sight of looking through a fire.

I will put into the box
The thirteenth month and the twenty fifth hour
A devil in the sky
An angel in Hell.

I will swim in my box
And lay on the yellow beach
And when I'm lonely I will always go into my box.

Ben Houghton (10)
Senacre Wood Primary School, Maidstone

Anthony

Indigo is the colour of the clouds
Flying above me,
You're the music drumming through my ears.

You're the cheese melting on my pizza,
The cranberries swelling around my glass.

You're the silk of my overgrown teddy,
The sun glazing down on me.

You're the love of my life

You're the horizon drifting by me
The palm trees swaying in the wind.

You're the boat drifting me out to sea,
The stars dancing in the night sky.

You're the butterfly fluttering from tree to tree,
The grasshopper leaping from leaf to leaf.

You're the moment I swim in a relay and win.

Alice Manser (11)
Senacre Wood Primary School, Maidstone

My Dad

You're like the red army kit of England
You're like Eminem rapping his songs
You're like pizza going down my throat
You're the best dad ever
You're like Coke fizzing and slipping down my throat
You're like the smell of a leather jacket
You're like a Premier League football
You're the taste of chocolate bars
    Because
        You're
            My
                Dad!

Michael Mannell (11)
Senacre Wood Primary School, Maidstone

Midnight Games

Out of the toybox two by two
The teddies and toys come bouncing
Into the hallway quiet as mice
Watching out for the cat who comes pouncing.

Jumping each step
As they go down the stairs
Singing and dancing
Going in pairs.

Then one big, fat teddy
Opens the living room door
And they all run in shouting
Playing and lots more.

The rabbits are pop stars
Jumping on the spot
Some of them fall over
Losing the plot.

Dolls act like drama queens
Wearing pretty crowns
McDonalds toys just play around
Acting like clowns.

Then suddenly the fat bear
Switches on the light
Yelling 'Quick everyone
Get out of sight.'

They jump up the stairs
And into their bed
Waiting for the next night
Meanwhile resting their heads.

Kirsty Foster (11)
Senacre Wood Primary School, Maidstone

Weather

The sun is bright
And provides light,
The moon makes dark
Like a tree bark.

Snow is cold like ice
Solid as a dice
Clouds cause wet and soggy rain
So it's indoor play - such a pain.

Summer is the hottest
Winter is the coldest
There are lots of types of weather
It is very clever.

Anthony Luck (11)
Senacre Wood Primary School, Maidstone

My Mum

You're the sweetness of my sweet tea,
You're my eyes when I couldn't see,
You're the refreshing tropical juice,
That I gulp down.

You're like a silk velvet cover
That warms me up,
You're like the spice of my Chinese
Which burns my tongue.

Because you care, my happiness grows,
Like a beanstalk,
Climbing up and staying,
With me every day.

Samantha Craig (10)
Senacre Wood Primary School, Maidstone

I Will Put In My Hand
(Based on 'Magic Box' by Kit Wright)

I will put in my hand
The dazzling light of the sun
A tiger with a fin
A man on a moon.

I will put in my hand
The icy cold breeze of a polar bear's breath
A polar's hand touching a Chinese dragon
A freezing cold shed.

I will put in my hand
A chime in an ancient grandfather clock in an old palace
My cool dad picking me up
My two sisters walking to the shop.

I will put in my hand
A fish with wings and a fly with a shine
A monkey with a bark
A fish with a long leg.

I will put in my hand
The crunch of a crocodile's huge mouth
A boy in a dress
A girl with boxer shorts.

I will put in my hand
The smell of sea water
An old man talking fast
That's what I would put in my hand
What would you put in your hand?

Lewis Nicholson (11)
Senacre Wood Primary School, Maidstone

The Magic Heart
(Based on 'Magic Box' By Kit Wright)

I shall put in my heart
The meaning of love
The joy of scoring goals
The heart of my boyfriend.

I shall put in my heart
A monkey's cheeky grin
Helpfulness of my teacher
The soft texture of my teddy.

I shall put in my heart
The last ever touch of my jet-black rabbit
Laughter that I make
The last feel of my grandad's goatie.

I shall put in my heart
Blue sand and a purple sun
A shark bathing in a prickly nest
And a bird breaststroking in the sea.

My heart is full of love
In the corner emotion hides
The hinges are made out of care.

I shall swim in love
Inside my heart
Then think of my mum
And smile.

Natasha Tucker (11)
Senacre Wood Primary School, Maidstone

Late

Got up this morning
Bed screeched 'Snuggle under my warm duvet.'
'Can't' I said, 'Late.'

Went into the bathroom
Shower bellowed 'Have a wash, you smell.'
'Can't' I said, 'Late.'

Went into the kitchen
Kettle whistled 'Fill me up.'
'Can't' I said, 'Late.'

Went into the garden
Roses screamed 'Water me.'
'Can't' I said, 'Late.'

Went past the sweet shop
Jelly beans bounced 'Buy me.'
'Can't' I said, 'Late.'

Went to school
Teacher bellowed 'Come and learn lots of
Different subjects.'
'Can't' I said, 'Late.'

Craig Tupper (11)
Senacre Wood Primary School, Maidstone

Alfie

You're the scarlet in the flame
You're like Eminem in my ear
Your taste is a curry
You're the Alf in Alfie
You're the fizz in the Pepsi
Your clothes are Burberry
You're the grass in the Arsenal ground
You're the one who makes my belly tingle.

Jac Tompsett (11)
Senacre Wood Primary School, Maidstone

The Magic Box
(Based on 'Magic Box' by Kit Wright)

I will put in my box
A football with red stripes and black
Circles, a powerful kick will win the match
And the glory will start when they score.

I will put in my box
A computer, it is good for research,
And playing games, it amazes as well.

I will put in my box
A green tree and when it's summer all the
Leaves fall down.
In the spring all the leaves go back on the tree.

I will put in my box
The shining sun behind the wonderful clouds
Glancing to say hello.

I will put in my box
The sky is so beautiful with the clouds
And sun on so it makes the sky more shining.

Jay Kitchenham (10)
Senacre Wood Primary School, Maidstone

Favourite Things

You're the newborn tulip that smiles night and day.
Your hair is long and wavy, that gets more beautiful each day.

You're the sun in the sky which shines down on me,
You're the sugar in my cup of tea.

You're the magical presents under my tree,
You're the star in my life that makes me happy.

Lee Tucker (11)
Senacre Wood Primary School, Maidstone

The Magic Box
(Based on 'Magic Box' by Kit Wright)

I will put in my box
The softest cutest Labrador.
The sound of a robin chirping at spring.
The misty colour of a barn owl like
The early morning dawn.

I will put in my box
The frothy snow on a bare shivering tree.
The acrid smell of chlorine at the swimming pool.
Hair freshly washed with shampoo smelling of lemon.

I will put in my box
The rich feel of velvet and silk
The bubbling excitement of an impending holiday
Tantalising taste of cold ice cream and jelly.

I will put in my box
A tranquil river flowing up a mountain
The kiss of a breeze on a summer's day
Smell of fresh tasty baked bread.

My box is fashioned by gold, silver and ice.
With a moon on the lid and my pets in the corners
Its hinges are stars from the bluest sky.

I shall play in my box
With my family and friends on the clouds
Then rest under a shady tree
On the greenest freshest grass.

Jake Brown (11)
Senacre Wood Primary School, Maidstone

The Magic Box
(Based on 'Magic Box' By Kit Wright)

I will put in my box
The blazing sun peeping from behind a cloud
The last bite of the first shiny red cherry
The smell of fresh bread wafting my way.

I will put in my box
The sparkling trail of a slow silver snail
The last green leaf lying on a frosty bed of snow
The scurrying of a squirrel climbing a gnarled tree.

I will put in my box
The flow of the fire red, yellow and orange
The splash of the clearest water, touching my face
The flash of fast lightning whizzing through the night.

I will put in my box
A newborn baby with a full grown beard
A thirteenth season
And a twenty-fifth hour.

My box is fashioned from silver and gold
For protection
With happiness on the lid and love in the corners
The hinges are the claws of mice.

I shall dance on my box
On the sparkling polished stage
Then bow off daintily
With pride in my heart.

Zoe Woodcock (11)
Senacre Wood Primary School, Maidstone

Late

Got up this morning
Alarm clock buzzed 'Snooze'
'Can't' I said, 'Late.'

Went into the kitchen
Toaster clinked 'Feed me.'
'Can't' I said, 'Late.'

Went into the porch
Dog yelped 'Walk me.'
'Can't' I said, 'Late.'

Walked to the car
Car rumbled 'Leave me and walk.'
'Can't' I said, 'Late.'

Drove to lights
Traffic lights flashed 'Stop!'
'Can't' I said, 'Late.'

Walked towards work
Work building yawned 'Go home.'
'Can't' I said, 'Late.'

Got to desk
Drawers chattered 'Just in time.'
'Oh' I said, 'Not late.'

Jason Goodwin (11)
Senacre Wood Primary School, Maidstone

The Magic Heart
(Based on 'Magic Box' by Kit Wright)

I will put in my heart
A drop of morning dew from the sunny day,
Blue sparkling waves from the open sea,
Green giant trees swaying with the sun on a hot day.

I will put in my heart
Dolphins leaping in and out from the big blue ocean
An angel wearing devil's horns,
A devil wearing a halo.

I will put in my heart
Glittering stars from the night sky
A bright sun from the summer's day
All nine planets floating around its orbit.

I will put in my heart
A splash of a flowing river
A rainbow arching across the lands
Fields spreading across the Earth.

My box is fashioned with pearls and curls
With metal corners and a metal lock
With secrets spread all around.

I shall have discos and parties in my box
Listening to music and watching the coloured
Lights flashing and twirling around and around.

Emily Gilham (10)
Senacre Wood Primary School, Maidstone

In My Hole

I will put in my hole . . .
The largest cheese pie,
A fish with twelve colours
A gazelle with lots of energy.

I will put in my hole . . .
Two giant apples
An elephant with four tusks
A smile from the monkey's uncle.

I will put in my hole . . .
Two purple piranhas
A frog speaking to children
And nine delicious cherries.

I will put in my hole . . .
A thirty second day in a month
A dolphin that speaks
And a human that eeks.

My hole is an eternal pit of memories
At the top it has a cluster of exquisite flowers
The inside is filled with happy and terrible thoughts
I will bungee-jump through my hole
Through mountains of China
And land softly on grass
The colour of laughing leaves.

James Manners (11)
Senacre Wood Primary School, Maidstone

Late

Got up this morning
Alarm screamed 'Press snooze'
'Can't' I said, 'Late.'

Went to kitchen
Sink dripping 'Turn me off'
'Can't' I said, 'Late.'

Went to front door
Letters chattering 'Open us,'
'Can't' I said, 'Late.'

Walked past Central Park
Trees swaying 'Sit down and relax
Let me fan you,'
'Can't' I said, 'Late.'

Passed a drink stall
Drinks fizzed 'I am as fizzy as can be,
Drink me.'
'Can't' I said, 'Late.'

Went past library
Book humming 'Read me,'
'OK,' I said, 'Not late.'

Chloe Penfold (10)
Senacre Wood Primary School, Maidstone

Frankenstein

Eats brains and bogies
And he has bolts in his head
And kills people.
I'd like to stay away
From Frankenstein.

Mark Ferrari (10)
Southwood Primary School, Dagenham

Spikey

Hedgehogs, hedgehogs
Rolling round
In a prickly ball
Along the ground
Under leaves
They like to sleep
Nice and snug
Nice and warm
Hedgehogs, hedgehogs
I love them so
How I wish I had one!

Sara Smith (10)
Southwood Primary School, Dagenham

School

I like school,
All the teachers are cool,
Art and PE really rule,
That's one of the reasons I like coming to school.

Miss Andrew is my teacher,
She is very nice,
She enjoys eating rice,
Miss Andrew teaches us a lot of cool stuff,
Her hair is as soft as fluff.

Mollie Sheridan (10)
Southwood Primary School, Dagenham

Miss Andrew

My teacher is so cool
That's why I love going to school,
She has such a nice smile,
And has so much style
My teacher . . . she rules!

Melisa Mert (10)
Southwood Primary School, Dagenham

The Chicken Nugget

The chicken nugget is just simply junk food
But you wouldn't realise the journey it takes
To get to your dinner plate.

What you do is *kill a chicken!*

Next you chop it down into bite size pieces
Last but not least you put on the breadcrumbs.

After all that work
Down the hatch.

Kurt Chilvers (10)
Southwood Primary School, Dagenham

My Pet Hamster

My pet hamster is brown and white
She sleeps in the day
And awake at night.
Her name is Fidget because she
Is never still.
Her favourite thing is to run in her wheel.

Amy Ebbs (10)
Southwood Primary School, Dagenham

West Ham

I like West Ham,
I am one of their fans
It would be good if we had Scholes,
Then I would be shouting 'Goal!'

Adam Wiffen (9)
Southwood Primary School, Dagenham

My Bike

I like my bike
It's very red
I ride it up and down
I really wish my mum would let me ride it into town.

I ring my bell
Turn on the lights
Peddle as fast as I can
I like it when it's sunny because I can go round and round.

Taylor Paradise (10)
Southwood Primary School, Dagenham

Footie Fan

I like footie, it is great
I go with my mates and train till late.
We chase the ball at a fast rate.

Conor and Joe are the best I know.
When the ball comes watch them go,
The wind in their hair,
And light on their feet,
Now we know, the other team's beat!

James Boxall (10)
Southwood Primary School, Dagenham

I Love Cats

I love cats,
I wish they could hold bats,
So we could play tennis,
And act like a menace
Because I love cats.

Francesca Duffin (10)
Southwood Primary School, Dagenham

My Niece

As lovely as a rabbit
As sweet as a box of chocolates
As funny as a clown
As delightful as a flower
As pretty as a crystal
As playful as a dog
  My niece
    Is the best!

Charlie Pennington (8)
Southwood Primary School, Dagenham

My Sister

As clever as an inventor
As delightful as a cake
As friendly as a lamb
As kind as a cat
As pretty as a dolphin
As tall as a house
As helpful as a nurse
I love my sister!

Kathryn Smith (8)
Southwood Primary School, Dagenham

My Dad

As angry as a hulk
As hard as a rock
As lazy as a crocodile
As tall as a teacher
As moany as a mum.

    That's my dad!

Gus Hawkes (8)
Southwood Primary School, Dagenham

Death Of A Snowman

I was awake all night,
Big as a lonely bear,
Strong and firm and white
The black, tall hat I wear
Was draped with fluffy fur,
I felt so fit and well,
Till the world began to stir,
And the blazing sun swelled.
I was tired, began to yawn,
At nine in the setting sun,
I caught a chilly warm,
My nose began to run,
My hat grew floppy and fell,
Was followed by my melting
There was no warning bell,
But by night-time I was dead.

Roma Alcknaviciute
Southwood Primary School, Dagenham

My Friends

I'd be nothing without my friends
They are there for me and I'm there for them
Whenever I'm sad, they make me happy
When the day is bad, they make it great and chatty
I like my friends, they're really funny
Even when it's cloudy they make it all sunny
I'm really glad that I have friends
We'll stay friends until the end
They're great and they're good mates
They make me laugh and cry
We'll stay mates until we die.

Lauren Docherty (10)
Southwood Primary School, Dagenham

Dogs

Dogs, dogs
Bark at the cats
Sitting on the wall
Near a block of flats.

Dogs, dogs
Bark at the postman
Delivering the letters
In his shiny red van.

Dogs, dogs
Bark at the birds
Singing in the trees
Whistling the words.

Dogs, dogs
Barking at the bats
Out very late
Standing on a mat.

Katie Simpson (9)
Southwood Primary School, Dagenham

I Love Animals

I love animals, how cute they are.
Some live near, some live far.
Some live in trees, some underground,
Some of them hardly make a sound.
My favourite animal is a dog.
They fetch things small, like a tiny log.
Dogs will always be your friend
No matter how it turns out in the end!

Anna Smith (9)
Southwood Primary School, Dagenham

Dogs

Dogs, dogs
Bark at the cat
Sitting on a wall
Near the block of flats.

Dogs, dogs
Bark at the postman
Delivering the letters
In his shiny red van.

Dogs, dogs
Bark at the bird
Singing in the shade
Whistling the words.

Jerry Lewis (8)
Southwood Primary School, Dagenham

Alone

Scared
Scared
All on your own
Sitting on a sack in the black.

Lonely
Lonely
Is the little old man
Who lives on his own.

Frightened
Frightened
In the little old house
Sitting on his own.

Frank Griffin
Southwood Primary School, Dagenham

Alone

Scared, scared
Alone in the park
It's very dark inside the park.

Frightened, frightened,
I wish I could go home
I wish that I wasn't on my own.

Gloomy, gloomy
I'm all alone, it is night
I'm very scared, I feel a fright.

Tired, tired,
I want to go to bed,
I won't because something might creep
Up on my head.

Amazing, amazing,
Something has just happened
I open my eyes and I'm not in the
*Gloomy, dark
Park.*

Emileigh Day (9)
Southwood Primary School, Dagenham

My Cat

My cat Bluebell is very nice,
She goes in the garden and catches all the mice.
Her fur is as soft as silk,
She eats her food and drinks her milk.

She likes to play with my hair,
And then she sleeps on the chair.
I really love my little cat,
And I hope she knows that!

Sophie Arthur (10)
Southwood Primary School, Dagenham

Me And My Family

My name is Danni
My mum calls me super granny.

I have a brother called Jack
Who always moans about his back.

I have a mum
Who is pretty dumb.

I have a dad
Who goes pretty mad.

I have a pet fish
Who is called Tish.

That is all my family
Ain't they great?
I love them to bits
They're never late!

Danni Redgrave (11)
Southwood Primary School, Dagenham

My Nan

As kind as a cat
As soft as a toy
As nice as a dog
As happy as a Barbie doll
As quiet as a tree
As loving as a rose
As skinny as a rope
As helpful as a nurse

    That's my loving nanny!

Abigail O'Shea (8)
Southwood Primary School, Dagenham

The Monkey Gater

It was a dark, dank, dreadful night
And while millions were abed
The monkey gater woke itself
From a gunshot.

It was fatter than an elephant
Its teeth were sharper than a saw
The monkey gater was longer than two bits of wood.

It was quieter than a mouse
The moon was shining on the sea
The fish were scared of the monkey
The monkey gater wants a big tea.

Ross Worthing (11)
Southwood Primary School, Dagenham

My Girlfriend

As hot as an oven
As loving as a mum
As pretty as a flower
As beautiful as a dolphin
As helpful as a brother
As sweet as a puppy
As snuggly as a blanket
As friendly as a friend
    That's my girlfriend!

Ryan Bell (8)
Southwood Primary School, Dagenham

Me and My Family

My name is Kerry
I'm as tall as a cherry.

My sister's name is Jo
She has a very big toe.

My brother's name is John
His feet pong.

I have a mum
Who is pretty dumb.

I have a dad
Who is quite sad (boo hoo).

I have two kittens called
Micky and Mittens.

That is my family
Don't we sound dandy!

Kerry Davies (11)
Southwood Primary School, Dagenham

Friends

My friends are the best,
Better than the rest.
We like the same books,
We like the same looks.
Sometimes we break up
But we always make up.
We are always stuck together,
We will always keep in touch forever.

Rachel Ellis (10)
Southwood Primary School, Dagenham

Alone

Sad
Sad
Is the little young man
Who lives in an igloo.

Lonely
Lonely
He's lonely without
His friends.

Bored
Bored
Nothing to do
Not even chasing
A fly.

Jay Wheeler (9)
Southwood Primary School, Dagenham

My Sister

As crazy as a monkey
As lazy as a pig
As tall as a giraffe
As delightful as a cream cake
As slim as a pencil
As annoying as a cat
As moany as a baby
As pretty as a pony
    That's my sister!

Kate Wallace (8)
Southwood Primary School, Dagenham

The Monkydile

It was a dark, dank, dreadful night
And while millions were abed
The monkydile swung through the trees
'I must find some food' it said.

It swung into the town very quietly
It was as tall as an elephant
It was as long as three houses
It marched like a giant ant.

It was taller than the Twin Towers
More massive than three hundred men lined up
Its teeth so sharp and pointy
Its back so scaly and tough.

Sarah Jones (10)
Southwood Primary School, Dagenham

My Nan

As peaceful as a person
As thin as a snake
As thankful as a dinosaur
As helpful as a mum
As pretty as a kitten
As soft as a budgie
As cuddly as a teddy bear
As delightful as a girl.
    I love my nan.

Georgie Read (8)
Southwood Primary School, Dagenham

Camping

Here we go!
Getting in the car
Saying our goodbyes,
'Taaa-raaa.'

We're on the open road now.
We saw horses, donkeys and a cow.
I found my drink at the back
I also had a packet of Nic-Naks.

After a long journey, we're finally here,
At the empty site of Sevoly Dear.
'What a lovely camp' I said.
But we spent the day making the beds.

The next day came and I made breakfast
I made eggs, bacon and chips.
We had melon afterwards
But I swallowed some of the pips.

Now we've got to go to bed again
The cockerel was asleep, and so was the hen.
Anna was snoring very badly,
But I just sat there thinking proudly.

Gemma Smith (11)
Southwood Primary School, Dagenham

My Mum

My mum will always be there for me
Even though she can't climb a tree.
My mum child minds babies
It's really driving me crazy.
I do love my mum really,
That's why she'll always be there for me!

Kathryne Hamilton (10)
Southwood Primary School, Dagenham

Dogs

Dogs, dogs
Bark at the cats
Sitting on the wall
Near the block of flats.

Dogs, dogs
Bark at the postman
Delivering the letters
In his shiny red van.

Dogs, dogs
Bark at the birds
Singing in the shade
Whistling the words.

Dogs, dogs
Bark at the cats
Watching the rats.

Megan Little (9)
Southwood Primary School, Dagenham

Alone

I'm scared from the dark
Alleyway.

Scary
Scary

I wish all my family
Were here.

Alone
Alone

And they always say that
He lives on his own in a grange.

James Flexen-Tin (9)
Southwood Primary School, Dagenham

Dogs

Dogs, dogs
Bark at the cats
Sitting on the wall
Near the block of flats.

Dogs, dogs
Bark at the postman
Delivering the letters
In his shiny red van.

Dogs, dogs
Bark at the birds
Singing in the shade
Whistling the words.

Dogs, dogs
Bark at the rats
Sleeping on a mat
As fat as a cat.

Lewis Keble (10)
Southwood Primary School, Dagenham

West Ham

I support West Ham
I think I'm one of their number one fans
I've got all their stuff.
My mates think they're buff, but I don't.
My dad and brother like them so much.
They have a charm for luck
Which is their shirts which are dirty.
They think they're the best and so do I,
So will they be lifting up their vests while
Running around and shouting . . . *Goaaaal?*

Emily Richardson (10)
Southwood Primary School, Dagenham

Dogs

Dogs, dogs
Bark at the cats
Sitting on a wall
Near the block of flats.

Dogs, dogs
Bark at the postman
Delivering the letters
In his shiny red van.

Dogs, dogs
Bark at the birds
Singing in the shade
Whistling the words.

Dogs, dogs
Bark at the bees
Sitting in the trees
Watching all the fleas.

Luke Van Gelder (9)
Southwood Primary School, Dagenham

Haiku

Birds are flying high
Sun is shining in the sky
Waves are splashing hard.

Edward Searle (11)
Southwood Primary School, Dagenham

Haiku

Sea rocking gently
Curvy waves splashing slowly
An amazing scene.

Muhamet Halilaj (10)
Southwood Primary School, Dagenham

Dogs

Dogs, dogs
Bark at the cats
Sitting on the wall
Near the block of flats.

Dogs, dogs
Bark at the postman
Delivering the letters
In his shiny red van.

Dogs, dogs
Bark at birds
Singing in the shade
Whistling the words.

Dogs, dogs
Bark at the frog
Hopping past
With a little dog.

Mitchell Oxborrow (8)
Southwood Primary School, Dagenham

The Monkadon

It was a dark, dank, dreadful night
While millions were abed
The monkadon was up and awake
'I must get some food' he said.
It was as tall as a van
And as fat as a man
And he swings through the jungle like a chimpanzee
It swings through the jungle looking for food
And it will snatch whatever it sees.

Christopher Cooper (11)
Southwood Primary School, Dagenham

My Sister

As beautiful as a butterfly
As quiet as a fly
As loving as a mum
As calm as a cow
As sweet as a flower
As thankful as a person
As kind as a lamb
As friendly as a horse
    I love my sister!

Matthew Hamilton (8)
Southwood Primary School, Dagenham

My Dad

As cuddly as a cushion
As kind as my mum
As delightful as a kangaroo
As clever as an adult
As friendly as a dog
As sweet as a tweety bird
As old as an old man
As cool as Michael Owen.
    I love my dad.

Lewis Stevens (7)
Southwood Primary School, Dagenham

Summer Poem

Summer sun,
Summer sea,
Have fun,
For all to see.

The fresh air,
In the hot sun,
Burn and hurt,
Or tan in the sand.

Winter's far off,
So don't give up,
On the waves splashing,
And the sun shining.

Beth Willcocks (10)
Southwood Primary School, Dagenham

My Mum

As loving as my nanny
As caring as a god
As helpful as a teacher
As kind as an older sister
As cuddly as a teddy
As loud as an engine
As sweet as a flower
    That's my lovely mum!

Jordan Mabey (8)
Southwood Primary School, Dagenham

The Snakadon

It was a dark, dank, dreadful night
And while millions were abed
The snakadon stretched and slithered around
'I must find some food' he said.

It's longer than a metre ruler
As big as a car
Its teeth are as sharp as daggers
It slithered and hissed.

It slithered quietly through the cobbled streets
It curled up, saw people and very little cars go past
It uncurled and chased a man down the road
Then he ate the man.
The skanadon slithered back home to sleep.

David Crampton (11)
Southwood Primary School, Dagenham

My Mum Is

As kind as a butterfly
As thankful as a ladybird
As soft as a blanket
As cuddly as a bear
As respectful as God
As pretty as a queen
As delightful as afters
As sweet as a dolphin
As happy as a clown
    That's my loving mum!

Kirsty Simpson (8)
Southwood Primary School, Dagenham

The Crocohog

It was a dark, dank, dreadful night,
And while millions were abed,
The crocohog was snarling,
Loud enough to wake the dead.

Taller than a house,
More massive than a tree,
It crawled and slithered around,
It moved as quiet as you or me.

His head so very spiky,
His face quite ugly too,
His eyes could see for miles
He could even see me and you.

Michael Howes (11)
Southwood Primary School, Dagenham

My Little Sister

As crazy as a lion
As slim as a ruler
As friendly as a puppy
As pleasant as a forever friend
As kind as a butterfly
Sometimes as mean as a tiger
As crazy as a little devil
As beautiful as a princess
    That's my little sister!

Abigail Davies (8)
Southwood Primary School, Dagenham

Seasons

Spring, spring
Flowers growing
Lambs getting ready to be born.

Summer, summer
Warm air
People go on hot holidays.

Autumn, autumn
Leaves coming off the trees
Red, brown, orange, so lovely to see.

Winter, winter
Arrives,
Build a snowman.
Paige Berrecloth (9)
Southwood Primary School, Dagenham

My Sister

As clever as a scientist
As delightful as a knickerbocker glory
As respectful as my mum
As beautiful as a princess
As sweet as a baby
As small as a flower pot
As thin as a ballerina
As soft as a feather.
    I love my sister!
Jennifer Smith (8)
Southwood Primary School, Dagenham

Fish

Big fish, little fish
Fish everywhere.
They're in my pond,
And I stand and stare.
They're my favourite water creatures,
Because their bodies are wonderful features.

Ellie Terry (9)
Southwood Primary School, Dagenham

Haikus

The dull racoon eats
Nibbling, chewing and biting
Racoon is hungry.

The moody calm sea
Overlapping and noisy
Blue waves travel fast.

Arif Hossain (11)
Southwood Primary School, Dagenham

Haiku

Sea smashing up rocks
Water swaying back and forth
Plane falls from above.

Luke Bartolo (11)
Southwood Primary School, Dagenham

My Brother

As thankful as my sister
As strict as a headteacher
As horrible as a shark
As angry as my sister
As lazy as a crocodile
As loud as an instrument
As crazy as a clown
As mean as a tiger
    That's my brother!

Hammad Khan (7)
Southwood Primary School, Dagenham

My Mum

As soft as a sponge
As calm as a god
As tall as a building
As delightful as a Turkish Delight
As loud as a child
As strict as a teacher.

    That's my mum!

Ben Skinner (8)
Southwood Primary School, Dagenham

My Dad

As hard as a rock
As lazy as a crocodile
As tall as a giraffe
As moany as an elephant
As smart as a scientist
As clever as a discoverer
    That's my dad!

John Cooper (8)
Southwood Primary School, Dagenham

My Sister

As thin as a stick
As loud as music
As quick as a car
As cute as a baby
As cuddly as a teddy bear
As nice as my mum
As sweet as a doll
As clever as a teacher
    That's my sister!

Millennia Severino (8)
Southwood Primary School, Dagenham

My Brother

As funny as a clown
As loving as my whole family put together
As tall as a flat
As sharp as a calculator
As cuddly as a big teddy bear
As happy as a peaceful old man
As easily annoyed as a teenager
As crazy as a chimpanzee
    That's my kind loving brother!

Liam Peters (8)
Southwood Primary School, Dagenham

My Mum

As soft as a bear
As crazy as a monkey
As lovely as a queen
As noisy as a train
As helpful as a helper
As friendly as children
As sweet as a baby.
    That's my mum!
    My mum is the best!

Zaid Jilani (8)
Southwood Primary School, Dagenham

My Brother

As kind as my mum
As helpful as a robot
As friendly as my friends
As thin as a root
As happy as a clown
As proud as my dad
As jolly as a pirate.
    That's my only brother!

Alfie Yeaman (8)
Southwood Primary School, Dagenham

My Friend

As friendly as a dog
As noisy as a lion
As silly as a monkey
As big as a jackal
As mental as a tiger
    That's my friend!

Sam Berrecloth (7)
Southwood Primary School, Dagenham

The Seasons

Springtime with beautiful green leaves
And tiny thick shoots.

Summertime with the hatching wildlife
And wonderful flowers.

Autumn time with falling leaves
And shorter days.

Wintertime with flying to the south
And a shiny, white Christmas.

Daniel Challis (9)
Southwood Primary School, Dagenham

Pussy Cat

Oh pussy cat, oh pussy cat
What are you looking at?
Sitting on the wall all day
Waiting for me to come and play.

Lazing in the sun
Waiting for some fun
Here comes a dog
Oh pussy cat
Where have you gone?

Lauren Morley (9)
Southwood Primary School, Dagenham

My Mum

As crazy as a monkey
As tasteful as a sweet
As cuddly as a bear
As thankful as a skivvy
As lovely as a queen
As caring as a lord
As friendly as a friend
    That's my mum!

Macaulay Harrison (8)
Southwood Primary School, Dagenham

Once Upon A Time

O nce upon a time, a million years ago
N o golf was made, until this day
C alled a caveman
'E veryone, I've got a game to play.'

U nder a pit a round pebble lay
P utted the pebble, not far at all
O ut of luck he shouted out
N one of this is working out.

A caveman growled and snarled

'T his isn't my lucky day
I try too hard
M y club won't hit
E very ball goes astray.'

Matthew Seman (8)
The Westborough Primary School, Westcliff-on-Sea

Once Upon A Rhyme

To look up at the clouds and watch them pass by
Up in the blue blue sky
Where the birds will sing
And diamonds will ring,
Up in that blue blue sky.

To hear the band whilst
Laying on the soft, soft sand.
Golden and yellow
Everyone feels mellow,
Laying on that soft, soft sand.

To watch and be
Down on the blue, blue sea.
The water that flows from left to right,
It is dark in the night
Down on that blue, blue sea.

Anastasia Chinery (10)
The Westborough Primary School, Westcliff-on-Sea

Pilot Fancy

Pilot one, start the jet,
And make it good so I can win the bet!
Pilot two, rocket ends,
Twist and turn around the bends!
Pilot three, turn on the smoke,
And make me a drink of brandy and Coke.
Pilot four, land the jet!
Hooray for me I've won the bet!
What! You want half?
Don't be silly; you're having a laugh!
Paying you is bad enough, for just doing
All this fancy stuff!

Natasha Stone (10)
The Westborough Primary School, Westcliff-on-Sea

The Zoo

I went to the zoo
What shall I do?
Look at the animals
And see what is new.

There are lions and wolves
Elephants and bears
I will look for the
Animals in their lairs.

There are giraffes and camels
Monkeys and penguins
And even tropical fish
Swimming with their fins.

There are parrots and lizards
Snakes and spiders
And keepers with food
Feeding the tigers.

There are apes and insects
Pandas and seals
At home time I will
Pay for my toy panda at the tills.

Helena Layzell (8)
The Westborough Primary School, Westcliff-on-Sea

Autumn

Leaves swirling and twirling
Like a twister turning
The wind going round
Like wolves howling and growling
Empty trees with no leaves just sitting there
Little squirrels just standing around freezing cold
Like little statues dotted around.

Lauren Fryer (10)
The Westborough Primary School, Westcliff-on-Sea

The Top Of The Hill

I was at the top
Of the hill
I was counting
3 2 1 – *go!*
Before I knew it
I was off,
Rolling and twirling
Like a tornado
Weeee!
Faster and faster,
Picking up speed.
I was very dizzy,
Almost sick.
It was going on forever,
I was finally slowing down.
I reached the bottom.
I had time . . .
For one more go!

Jack Quy (8)
The Westborough Primary School, Westcliff-on-Sea

Broken Foot

B roken foot, broken foot!
R ight or left, which one is it?
O n the team playing well
K icking the ball to my mates
E qualiser need it soon or we've lost!
N ow or never, we've got to win.

F oot is broken, foot is broken!
O h no, my foot is sore!
O h no, my foot is sore!
T eam has lost the match, all my fault!

Alex Jones (11)
The Westborough Primary School, Westcliff-on-Sea

The Ant Killer

Scooting around
On my scooter
As fast as I could
In my back garden
Not thinking about life
At first actually, accidentally
I ran over an ant.

I felt sorry and ashamed
Of myself
Then I got into the habit,
Joyfully squashing ants
I did it to every one
In sight
I smiled secretly
Feeling pleased with myself.

As I got older
And fonder of ants
I noticed the destruction
That I was causing
A shiver went right
Down my spine,
I felt the importance of life
I looked at the bloodstained
Wheels of my scooter
In disgust.

Hollian Gibbs-Leake (8)
The Westborough Primary School, Westcliff-on-Sea

I'm Scared

There's something upstairs
I don't know who's there
I think it's big and hairy
I think it's really scary
I'm creeping upstairs
I'm finding out who's there
I think it's in my room
It's going boom, boom.
I rush into my room and
What do I find?
I find a little spider in my blinds.
Is that all it was?
I'm very confused
But I hope next time I'll find something good.

Rachel Ellis (8)
The Westborough Primary School, Westcliff-on-Sea

Winter Woman

Winter eats autumn away
With her rough skin
Taking the leaves
Her scruffy hair whirling
In the chilly wind
And blowing in her face.

Here comes the winter woman
Flowing through the forest
Stripping the trees bare
Riding on her ice chariot.
Her icicle fingers scraping the trees
And bringing winter in.

Benjamin Cooper (9)
The Westborough Primary School, Westcliff-on-Sea

Once Upon A Rhyme

My brother is a nuisance
He plays horrible games
He tries to tie me up
And calls me nasty names.

My mummy heard him do this
She ordered him to stop
My brother thinks he's clever
But clearly he's not.

Jade Butler (9)
The Westborough Primary School, Westcliff-on-Sea

Sounds

The clock goes tick
The stairs start to creak
The window starts to rattle
As the wind starts to speak.

The bees are buzzing
The trees are rustling
The washing is wanting to come in.

Megan Said
The Westborough Primary School, Westcliff-on-Sea

The Jungle

In the jungle monkeys are screeching,
Leopards are jumping, snakes are slithering at my feet.
I see a parrot in a tree squawking.
'Squawk' he said to me
Tigers are roaring, lions are yawning
Now I'm here I am not making a sound
I hear a cheetah running around.

Poppy Aubrey (8)
The Westborough Primary School, Westcliff-on-Sea

Ocean Sounds

Birds are singing
Dolphins squeaking
Penguins flapping
Sharks chewing
Fish swishing
Boat engine's purring
Sea sploshing
Whales whooing
'Help!' shouts the man overboard.

Josh Mendes (8)
The Westborough Primary School, Westcliff-on-Sea

Sounds Outside

The buzzing of a bee
The bang of a gun
The bang of a tank
The rustling of a tree
The clank of a brake
The bang of a piston
The isss of a snake
The tick of a clock.

William Summers (8)
The Westborough Primary School, Westcliff-on-Sea

Dry Land Sounds

The trample of a buffalo
The blazing of the sun
The rumble of an earthquake
The crack of the floor
The grumble of a rocket launch.

Joseph Jordan (8)
The Westborough Primary School, Westcliff-on-Sea

My Garden Sounds

The birds are cheeping
And the bushes are creeping
My dad's hammer bangs
And the washing hangs
My ball is bouncing and
My little brother's pouncing
And it's really cool in the swimming pool.
While the clock is ticking
My brother can't stop kicking a ball,
And that's all.

Shannon Dorrington (8)
The Westborough Primary School, Westcliff-on-Sea

Sea Sounds

The swish of a shark's tail
The sting of a jellyfish
And the gurgle of a whale.
The swish of a fish
The splash of a seagull
The electrifying shock of an eel
A flock of plankton
A splash of a seal.

Charles Deebank (8)
The Westborough Primary School, Westcliff-on-Sea

Snowy Child

Thin brown trees appear, bringing coldness and snow,
Snowflakes covering the windy sky.
Icy silvery feet stamp on the crunching floor.
It's a thin crispy girl blowing the grey air
With a sharp breath into crinkly faces of white.

Caroline Howe (9)
The Westborough Primary School, Westcliff-on-Sea

The World

The world is a sphere
A big round sphere
The grass is green
A voice is never seen
The clouds are white
And the sea is blue.

The world rotates
Round and round
Do you hear the
Sound of the wind
Blowing hard,
The birds singing and
The church bells ringing?

The people are happy,
Smiling, laughing,
Dancing and prancing
The children are learning
Earning education.

Some children are playing
While others are praying for God
To help them in
Everything they do.

Tanaka Mutonono (11)
The Westborough Primary School, Westcliff-on-Sea

Earth

E very day greenhouse gases build up, our
A ir is getting polluted
R ain is turning to acid
T he Earth we live in is dying
H elp to save it now.

Emmanuel Gbegli (11)
The Westborough Primary School, Westcliff-on-Sea

The Woodcutter

Deep in the wood
In the dark there stood
A woodcutter walking along.

He was walking around
And found a hat on the ground
Left it and went his way.

He was walking all alone
When he saw a purse on a stone
He left it and went on his way.

He was limping along because he hurt his knee
Then he saw some rope hanging from a tree
He left it and went on his way.

He was looking around when he stumbled and fell
And ran into a body that looked like Hell
And he screamed and ran away.

Sam Sage (10)
The Westborough Primary School, Westcliff-on-Sea

The Moonlight

The moonlight is the spotlight
It's the darkness of the sky
Night sky is so dark for us
We can't see a thing at all
But the cats . . .
They can see nearly everything
Because their eyes are extra good
I watch the stars in the sky
Plus the moon as well
They are so pretty
Yet so far away, I can see them
I see a twinkle in the corner of my eye.

Rachael King (11)
The Westborough Primary School, Westcliff-on-Sea

Seasons

Winter is a white blanket covered in sugar which is spread
Over the life of colour.
Winter is a silver linen hung over the blue sky.
Animals hide away and rest until the warm spring returns.

Autumn is rustling leaves covering the green grass
And when white blossoms fall.
Autumn is when children play in woollen jumpers and cotton hats
And jump in red and brown leaves which crunch under their feet.

Spring is when the flowers bloom and blossoms blossom
Animals crawl from their beds and lambs are shaved,
And the leaves are green again.

Summer is the sun coming to play
And the grey linen is pulled from the sky.
People sit under trees and fan themselves
And enjoy picnics in the park.
Young lovers walk in the park at midnight
After a day of sun,
They sit on a bench and eat truffles
As the cycle of seasons flow . . .

Emily Summers (10)
The Westborough Primary School, Westcliff-on-Sea

My Big Brother

My big brother is funny
My big brother is great
My big brother loves money
My big brother sometimes I hate.

Samantha Harrold (8)
The Westborough Primary School, Westcliff-on-Sea

The Pain

I was running, running,
After school.
Suddenly I couldn't feel the ground.
I was falling
Down
Down
Down.
I felt lots of pain.
It felt like broken glass,
Smashed into my face
It felt really bad.
I ran to the medical room
With a bleeding nose.
I had to go to hospital
I couldn't eat.
I was hungry, so, so hungry
My dad bought me
A Game Boy.
It cheered me up,
A bit
That's all I remember.

Louis Hosking (8)
The Westborough Primary School, Westcliff-on-Sea

My Limerick

There once was a boy called Josh,
Who was awfully, awfully posh.
He lived in a palace
With his wife called Alice
And her cat died
So my wife and I cried.

Joshua Ross (10)
The Westborough Primary School, Westcliff-on-Sea

Fred

Fred
Is dead
He landed on his head
But now he's lying
On the ground
In a flower bed.

He fell
And fell
And splattered on the floor
But now he's lying in a box
With a bolted door.

When he landed there
Blood went everywhere
It went in people's eyes
(Even in their flies!)
That was the song of Fred
Because now
Fred is dead.

Alexander Turpin (11)
The Westborough Primary School, Westcliff-on-Sea

Once Upon A Rhyme . . .

I was having a lovely time
In the land of nod
Eating something odd
It was rather smelly
It looked like jelly
But tasted like cream
Then I woke up and it was all a dream.

Emma Davies (11)
The Westborough Primary School, Westcliff-on-Sea

Once Upon A Rhyme

Once upon a rhyme, I found a magical place
Where fairies danced
And sprinkled dust as if they were tranced.

Once upon a rhyme, I found a magical place
Where princesses were freed
From evil witches.

Once upon a rhyme I found a magical place
Where swans swam in the river
And flew at their own pace.

Once upon a rhyme I found a magical place
Where everyone was friends
And always stayed friends.

Katrina Wakeling (10)
The Westborough Primary School, Westcliff-on-Sea

The Witch

Once upon a time
There was an ugly witch
Which flew into my room
And nicked a piece of string.

She had a long black cloak
With a tall pointy hat,
A very long broomstick
In the shape of a bat.

She gave an evil laugh
Without a thought
Then hopped back on her broom
And flew right out.

Justine Jefferies (11)
The Westborough Primary School, Westcliff-on-Sea

The Boy Who Loved To Rhyme

Once upon a time
There was a boy who loved to rhyme
He rhymed at home, he rhymed at school
He even rhymed at his brother's funeral.
But one day he got a rhymer's block
He couldn't think of a rhyme, and even put on one of his socks.

This went on for days,
Even at his favourite theatre plays,
He thought his rhyming days were over,
So he wanted to start a new life in Dover.

When he was sitting in his garden at night
He saw a beautiful sight
No, not the next-door neighbour's new flash car,
But a shooting star.
He wished if he could rhyme again
And also if he could own Big Ben.
Suddenly he began to rhyme,
And had a wonderful time
But drove his mum round the bend.

Luke Savidge (11)
The Westborough Primary School, Westcliff-on-Sea

Autumn Days

Looking up in the sky reminds me of sparkles
Like vanishing stars.
With fireworks going off like bombs at night.
With a wet, rainy, bright bit of rainbow
With a strong smell of greasy chips wrapped in paper
Like a skin.

Robert Heathcote (11)
The Westborough Primary School, Westcliff-on-Sea

Autumn

I looked outside
The sky was as dark as
A black hole.
I snuggled down for my extra
Hour in bed,
Trying to keep warm.

Hearing the wind brushing
The leaves
Up! Up! In the air,
Birds are singing like pop stars
Then I heard the wind again
Walking down the street
Pushing the leaves out of
The way.

James Middleton (10)
The Westborough Primary School, Westcliff-on-Sea

Fairy Reunion

Magical, fantasy, dreams and more,
Fairies and witches and trolls galore.
Mix them together and what do you find?
A home-made poem with lots of lines!
Humpty's on there with a mobile phone,
And little Miss Muffet's starting to groan.
Little Bo Peep has found her sheep
And now is trying to go to sleep
But with all the noise of Captain Hook
Shouting and groaning 'cause he can't cook.
Magical, fantasy, dreams and more
Fairies and witches and trolls galore,
Mix them together and what do you find?
A home-made poem with no more lines!

Lydia Ellis (10)
The Westborough Primary School, Westcliff-on-Sea

Autumn

Leaves crunching under your feet
They're crying for help
The burning smell
Of bonfire night
The foggy atmosphere
Is like a ghostly world
See fantastic and colourful fireworks
Always remember, remember
The fifth of November.
The autumn air whistling
Calling people to attention
Hallowe'en is here
The devils have landed
I come home
Waiting for another autumn.

Gemma Larking (11)
The Westborough Primary School, Westcliff-on-Sea

The Sweets!

Crunch! Crunch! Crunch!
Go the sweets.
Raspberry, strawberry, chocolate and mint
Gone as quick as a wink,
All my favourite sweets gone
Before you even blink.
Sugar coated chocolate sweets!
Yum! Yum! Yum!
I go to the shop to buy some more
But they're all gone, bum!

Carrie Beckett (11)
The Westborough Primary School, Westcliff-on-Sea

The Seasons

The summer sun shining bright
So warm and light.
The golden sand and the deepest blue sea
Is enough of paradise for me.

The autumn sky dull and grey
So cold I stay in bed all day
The golden leaves lay on the floor
Crunch, crunch, crunch, I crunch some more.

The spring flowers yellow and bright
The world seems so full of light.
The huge luscious fields of green
I feel so happy not at all mean.

The winter floor frozen with ice
The landscape feels so nice
The plants lay dead on the floor
No colour shows anymore.

The seasons change from hot to cold
With all this excitement you never feel old.

Alex Lawrence (11)
The Westborough Primary School, Westcliff-on-Sea

My Limerick

There was a girl called Nicole
Who lived in a very messy hole.
She would do the work
If only she could see through the murk
In her messy bedroom.

Her mum bought her a broom
For Nicole's bedroom
But there was something about the broom
Nicole cast a spell and made a smell
Which made it a whole lot worse
Than before the room was tidy.

Nicole Drumm (11)
The Westborough Primary School, Westcliff-on-Sea

Once Upon A Rhyme

Wizards and witches cast a spell
Sometimes it makes a horrible smell
Things go crazy in fantasy land
Like a very rubbish band
Crackling windows and much more
Leaving some people on the floor.

Some place else, somewhere quieter,
It is a lot nicer and brighter
So if you're looking for somewhere to sleep
This is the place with rhymes and sheep
The old woman who lived in a shoe
Now she didn't have to 'shoo'
Her children are back from their trips
Now she can have fish and chips.

Mary is still quite contrary
She was friends with all the fairies
And old King Cole was a merry old soul
But he lost all his bowls
So now you've heard a poem from a king
Who had everything.

Rebecca Johnson (11)
The Westborough Primary School, Westcliff-on-Sea

My Limerick

There once was a young boy called Tom
Who was actually good at making bombs
He took one to school
Set it off in the hall
And now the whole place has gone.

Tom Hawkyard (11)
The Westborough Primary School, Westcliff-on-Sea

Seasons

Spring is flowers growing through greenness
It's the bare trees' endness
It's like a cannon shooting flowers
It's water glistening in the sunshine
It's rainbows appearing through the ever blue sky,
    That's spring.

Summer is the sun peeping through the cloudy skies
It's the end of darkness and the beginning of sunshine,
It's people at the beach playing in shiny sand,
It's the start of waterfights.
    That's summer.

Autumn is a thunderstorm which is raining leaves,
It's the beginning of gloomy evenings
It's like summer saying au revoir and winter saying a bientot.
    That's autumn.

Winter is plants hibernating from the winter's cold frost
It's your family buying new winter gear.
It's your mum persisting for you to eat warm food.
    That's winter.

Seasons change every year like people and their emotions.

Latoya Smith (10)
The Westborough Primary School, Westcliff-on-Sea

Giant Haiku

High and muscular
Tall as a high skyscraper
Hugely cloud breaking.

Waleed Moerat (11)
The Westborough Primary School, Westcliff-on-Sea

Living The Dream!

I'm living the high life
I've got everything to be seen
There's nothing wrong with my life
Living the dream!

I've got personal security
And the perfect cup of tea
I've got everything you could ask for
Living the dream!

I live in a ginormous mansion
In Florida by the sea
Which is where I like to splash my cash
Living the dream!

I like to live in style
With no one bothering me
There's nothing wrong with that I guess
Living the dream!

My hi-tech laser system
Turns on when I'm in bed
The feeling's green when I'm in safety
Living the dream!

I have all the modern electronics
But there's no time to see them all
All I can tell you is
That I'm
      Living the dream!

Katherine Ridley (11)
The Westborough Primary School, Westcliff-on-Sea

What Am I?

I am a goldfish
I am not gold
I'm orange
I'm an orange fish
I can't swim
I walk
I'm not a fish
I'm a camel.

I am a camel
I've got two humps on my back
I spit
I'm a brown camel
I can't walk
I sprint
I'm not a camel
I'm a cheetah.

I am a cheetah
I am yellow with brown spots
I run like the wind
I don't run
I sliver
And hiss
I'm not a cheetah
I'm a snake.

Ashley Webb (11)
The Westborough Primary School, Westcliff-on-Sea

Autumn

Autumn is when green leaves go yellow and brown
And the sun's face always has a frown.

When an icy hand touches your shoulder
And it's when the year turns colder and colder.

Jordan Hixon (11)
The Westborough Primary School, Westcliff-on-Sea

Boxing For Life

My favourite combination is jab jab hook
When Kev has a boxing match I have to look
Kev got knocked down by my little brother
He even gets boxed up by his mother
Me, Kev and Ryan go to the same boxing club
When we get home we head straight for the grub
I had a tournament in Margate
The boxer's name I had to fight was *Ricky 'The Rapid' Tate*
Bang, bang, bang, boom, now he's on the floor
All around the ring there is loads of blood and gore
We want to be Mike Tyson but we don't know how
If we smoke or drink we would be dead by now.

Tony Norton
The Westborough Primary School, Westcliff-on-Sea

Grandad

Walking down the street looking very neat,
Dressed in Sunday best.
With stick in hand he looks oh so grand
Top hat on head and suit of black.
He marched as if he was in a band
That grandad of mine his face all of a shine
Was going to the races to have a good time
Spending his pension and having fun
This old man never looks glum.
Looking happy and always glad
I'm so pleased he's my grandad.

Carl Ashbrook (11)
The Westborough Primary School, Westcliff-on-Sea

Boxing

My favourite sport is boxing.
I like to fight and get in the ring
Punching, sparring, training too
That's the boxing I like to do
Keeping fit is what it's all about
My boxing trainer likes to give a shout
His favourite shout is 'Get stuck in.'
If I don't do what he says I'll be in the bin
I like competitions 'cause I think I'm good
Because my mates come from the south west coast
But I come from
The Hood.

Kevin Lavery (11)
The Westborough Primary School, Westcliff-on-Sea

My Dogs

Not last night but the night before
My two dogs were scratching at the door
I went downstairs to let them in
They chewed up Mum's best rolling pin
The rolling pin was made of wood
My mum said they were not good
Then my mum said they were very bad
Then she got very mad
She put them in the shed
She said they had to go to bed
They barked and barked and made a din
So she had to let them both back in.

Simone Porter (11)
The Westborough Primary School, Westcliff-on-Sea

A Slimy Snail

About and around on the acorn tree

Sliver slime on the dark street road
Little house on the back of his back
Its hard, hard shell is swirly whirly
Movement not fast but really quite slow
Easy to squash but you have to wash your socks!
You can find a slimy snail anywhere.

Slippery slimy sluggish snail
Now they're asleep so dance on your feet
All they eat are your precious plants,
Crunching and munching around
I think they're cute so play the flute
Like a cuddly bear.

Rose-Marie Forward (10)
The Westborough Primary School, Westcliff-on-Sea

Autumn And Winter

The smell of autumn is quite tense
People paint a fence
The leaves are falling like empty sweet wrappers
The bugs are killed in a bug zapper
One day I went to Devon and had an extra
Hour in bed, it was Heaven.
The teens are out to drink and shout
In the morning flowers grow with a strong spout.
But now it's winter get your sledge
Fast now a hill at the speed of thirty
At the end of the day I'm wet and dirty.
In the house it's minus thirty.
I had a bath, now I'm not so dirty.

James Querney (11)
The Westborough Primary School, Westcliff-on-Sea

The Way I Live

The way I live is my choice
And I don't have much to give.
The way I live was a bless
And nothing less.

The way I live is a part of my life,
Included with a lot of strife.
I enjoy to play everyday
My life is a part of me
And many more things that I could see.

When I die I hope my friends and family will cry.
I'll always try the impossible before I die.

My father died before I was born.
I hope to see him another day
And my dreams of him will never go away.

Massie Mutonono (11)
The Westborough Primary School, Westcliff-on-Sea

Chocolate

Chocolate is glorious, it makes you feel like you're in Heaven
And it smells like Heaven.

You can feel it melting on your fingers.
When it melts it feels like you're melting with it
When it melts in your mouth.

It makes you feel warm and tingly inside.

Chocolate is nuts and crunch
And they all taste the same
Because chocolate is my favourite
    Sweet!

Catherine Roffey (11)
The Westborough Primary School, Westcliff-on-Sea

The Woodcutter

Walking down the path
Of the Japanese woods,
Is a woodcutter searching
For some good wood.
Climbing over logs
And trampling on leaves
He carries on walking until . . .
He stops.
There on a branch
Is a hat and some clothes,
He looks at them carefully
Then off he goes.
He carries on walking
And looking around,
Until he trips
Then looks on the ground.
There on the ground
Is a woven bag,
The woodcutter's worried
And also sad.
When he looks up
He saw something else.
A box on the ground
All by itself.
He starts walking forward
Then trips again
Looks on the ground
And sees someone dead.
He starts running away
And yelling like hell
He leaves the body alone
For the bees to dwell.

Max Piper (11)
The Westborough Primary School, Westcliff-on-Sea

Space Mountain

Next to me, was my grandad, his eyes were open,
But my eyes were shut.
It was a breathtaking ride,
The surroundings were scary.
The first loop was terrifying,
I gripped firmly on the bars,
It was a fast and furious ride
This was one heck of a ride
It would be a ride of a lifetime
    The Space Mountain.

Dean Butt (10)
The Westborough Primary School, Westcliff-on-Sea

The Old Man Of Bejing

There was an old man of Bejing
Who fell off his mother's swing
He fell on some pins
Which were filled with sins
That evil old man of Bejing.

Elliot Huxtable (10)
The Westborough Primary School, Westcliff-on-Sea

Battlefield Haiku

Fighting on the beach
Trenches near, troops advancing
Spiritual strength.

Lloyd Mallison (8)
Walgrave CP School, Northampton

Death War Haiku

Death is just away,
Always tired, hungry and sad.
When will this war end?

Florence Neilson (9)
Walgrave CP School, Northampton

Home Alone Haiku

My children have gone,
My poor husband might be dead
Why am I alone?

Iola McCorkindale (9)
Walgrave CP School, Northampton

The Doubts Of War Haiku

War is horrible
My air raid shelter is bad
I so hate Hitler.

Alex McCorkindale (9)
Walgrave CP School, Northampton

The Nightmare Haiku

Not willing to fight,
Scared to die, a mistake, dark,
In fear and horror.

Sofia Bonsor (10)
Walgrave CP School, Northampton

World War II

Smelly gas masks, scared
Sad, air raid shelters, hungry
Petrified, worried.

Ben Tout (9)
Walgrave CP School, Northampton

Never Knowing Haiku

Can you hear the bombs?
Screaming, shrieking, dropping fast
Spirits in the air.

Steven Percival-Clare (10)
Walgrave CP School, Northampton

The Torture Of War Haiku

I'm frightened and sad,
Worried, smelly and hungry,
Longing for a friend.

Laura Beckett (10)
Walgrave CP School, Northampton

Understanding Battles Haiku

Why has the world gone?
Will I be dead or alive?
Oh, how will it end?

Holly Bell (10)
Walgrave CP School, Northampton

Fighting Haiku

Fighting on the beach,
Tired, scared, alone, destroyed.
Trying to be brave.

Laura Howes (8)
Walgrave CP School, Northampton

Fading Unhappily

I feel upset now,
My life is fading away,
I want my time back.

Katie Worthington (10)
Walgrave CP School, Northampton

My Friend Lizzy

Lizzy went to another school
I miss her a lot.

Her soft and silky black curly hair,
All her funny jokes,
Her rosy cheeks and petal skin,
Her deep brown eyes like smoke,
Her sweaty hands hot as fire.

But Lizzy went to another school
I miss her a lot.

She's very bouncy happy and giggly,
She writes with her left hand,
She hated playing hockey,
But loved rounders and netball.

But Lizzy went to another school
I miss her a lot.

Juliet Sparrow (9)
Winchester House School, Brackley

My Guinea Pig Honey

*Honey's dead
And I'm sorry about that.*

She'd silk fur,
Shone in the sun,
Was never naughty,
Had ruby eyes,
A little piglet nose.

*Honey's dead
And I'm sorry about that.*

She used to squeak,
She used to squeal,
Her knobbly legs,
So short, so thin,
But ever so strong.

*Honey's dead
And I'm sorry about that.*

Claws so sharp,
But it never hurt,
Scratching post in the corner,
But never used,
It was brand new.

*Honey's dead
And I'm sorry about that.*

Her ears so soft,
Like pieces of silk,
Warm in my hands,
Like a blazing fire.

*Honey's dead
And I'm sorry about that.*

Alice Wood (10)
Winchester House School, Brackley

Grandpa

I never saw my grandpa
He died before I was born

He had a chair that went up the stairs
A curly, white mass of hair
Deep brown enormous eyes.

I never saw my grandpa
He died before I was born

He died of very bad cancer
He had a big green leather coat
Loose and worn inside.

I never saw my grandpa
He die before I was born

With the handkerchief I still have
The big black holey boots
And the enjoyment I never had.

Sophie Scott (10)
Winchester House School, Brackley

Cookie

Cookie's passed away and I'll
Always remember her.

Cookie had ginger patches, black patches.
The colour was so clear, she used to purr like
A tractor and curl up on an armchair.

Cookie's passed away and I'll
Always remember her

I would sit down on a chair and she would be
Lingering there. She would sit on my lap and
Had a great appetite for food.

Cookie's passed away and I'll
Always remember her.

James Rudkin (9)
Winchester House School, Brackley

Bella

Now Bella's gone,
And I miss her.

Silvery white coat
Like ice, flowing
Mane and tail.

Now Bella's gone,
And I miss her.

Beautiful kind eyes
That fill you with happiness,
Delicate feet
Like snowflakes.

Now Bella's gone,
And I miss her.

Light footsteps, like
A panther when hunting;
Proud as a lion;
Feathered fetlocks, soft as silk.

Now Bella's gone,
And I miss her.

Prancing like a stag
When she walks, shies
At little things, like
A squirrel from afar.

Now Bella's gone,
And I miss her.

Sweet as a kitten,
Beautiful as a fairy,
Ears prick at any small
Sound.

Now Bella's gone,
And I miss her.

A high pitched whinny
Like a scream in a forest,
A galloping ghost in
The night.

*Now Bella's gone,
And I miss her.*

Tabitha Owen (10)
Winchester House School, Brackley

Ralphy

*Ralphy was eighteen
And that was that.*

He used to bark all the time.
He had dark spots and the rest was yellow.
He was an Airedale.
And he was special.
He had always had a limp.

*Ralphy was eighteen
And that was that.*

One eye was blue and the other was black.
And he used to chew the potato sack.
He loved to jump in the pool.
When he got out his fur looked all cool.
He loved licking you and smelling you.
And his tongue was soft and it tickled you.
And his nose was wet, soggy and black.

*Ralphy was eighteen
And that was that.*

Georgia Mossman (10)
Winchester House School, Brackley

Great Grandpa

My grandpa died
When I was two.
My mum was sad and I was too.
Lived in Lancashire
Wore trousers high up
His grey hair
Was greasy as chips
He was an inventor
Who loved golf.
He had great stories
That I really liked
Rough hands,
Smelt of plants
My grandpa died
When I was two
So come back Grandpa I really miss you.

Ned Kingdon (9)
Winchester House School, Brackley

Rupert

Rupert had a kind face and eyes with globes all around them.
His lips never told secrets or gave away his feelings.

Rupert's gone and I'm sad about that.

He was a sporty little boy who was very good at footie.
I recall he liked sliding down the banister
He liked to be around the stairs and play outside.
His favourite sport was skiing he had been on quite a few trips
His second favourite was football but now I'll call it quits.

Rupert's gone and I'm sad about that.

Oscar Cole (10)
Winchester House School, Brackley

My Friend

*Olivia's moved away
And I feel sad about that.*

She had brown long straight hair;
She was friendly and small
She was funny and giggly.

*Olivia's moved away
And I feel sad about that.*

She had blue eyes
She was a tanned girl
She smelled like a flower
And she was very playful.

*Olivia's moved away
And I feel sad about that.*

She wore lots of dresses
She liked books and
She loved toys.

*Olivia's moved away
And I feel sad about that.*

Sarah Warner (10)
Winchester House School, Brackley

My Old Dog Bruleigh

He had a long furry tail,
He didn't hurt you at all
And that's why I love him for,
He's the best of all.

*Bruleigh's gone and
I wish he'd come back.*

We only had him for two days,
Because my dad didn't approve,
So we lost him,
He wouldn't scratch you at all,
For he's the best of all.

*Bruleigh's gone and
I wish he'd come back.*

His eyes would glare and stare at you,
He'd pant and puff if he had enough,
And I love him for who he is,
And that is Bruleigh, my old dog.

Charlie Winton (10)
Winchester House School, Brackley

My Grandpa

Grandpa had a heart attack;
He died and now I'm sad.

I loved his funny jokes.
His nose was small
And crooked.
His bright blue eyes
Were such a surprise.

Grandpa had a heart attack;
He died and now I'm sad.

His hair was brown and tough,
His voice was kind and rough;
He lived nearby;
He smelled of mints.

Grandpa had a heart attack;
He died and now I'm sad.

Joe Tusting (10)
Winchester House School, Brackley

Minny Was Sold

*Minny was sold
And my friend was gone.*

A huge hairy body
Soft, like a hamster;
Spiky ears,
Greeny-brown tree bark eyes
That shone.
Soft breath in my face,
Nuzzles me away
In a friendly way.

*But Minny was sold
And my friend was gone.*

Liked his food;
Pony nuts in metal bowl
Rattled round.
Got excited
Loved his freedom;
Didn't like being caught.

*But Minny was sold
And my friend was gone.*

Was very strong
And speedy too.
Mane and tail
Were light brown
That's my friend
And he's gone.

*Minny was sold
And my friend was gone.*

Emily Taylor (9)
Winchester House School, Brackley

My Dad Moved

My dad moved away from home,
I felt sad and angry about that.

He tells me jokes and stories,
I have heard all six of them,
Over and over again.
His voice booms like thunder.
His deep blue eyes, when I stare into
Them I dream.
His hair is as wiry as a broom,
And nearly bald.
His ears are floppy and big like a giraffe.
He has got black hairs in his nostrils.
He is patient, most of the time.

My dad moved away from home
I felt sad and angry about that Dad.

He gives our cat pork scratchings sometimes.
His hands can nearly fit around my head.
His house smells of cat food.
He goes down to the pub sometimes,
Mostly at night.

My dad moved away from home
I felt sad and angry about that.

Ben Strong (10)
Winchester House School, Brackley

Teasel

*Teasel's gone,
I'm sad to say.*

My dog died, her name was Teasel.
She was a small Jack Russell terrier,
Teasel had a coat like a full leafed tree.
She would chase a bee;
Round and round the tree,
She played with Panda around the garden.

*Teasel's gone
I'm depressed to say.*

Teasel slept in a very smelly bed;
It looked an uncomfortable position.
She played football with my brothers and me;
Came riding with my family;
We scattered her ashes in the shady bed.

*Teasel's gone
I'm annoyed to say.*

Archie Smyth-Osbourne (10)
Winchester House School, Brackley

Soda

She was quite chubby
Her legs moved very fast
Her mouse collection was as full as a double decker
That ginger, black and white.

Soda was old
So that was that.

Also she had a short stubby tail
Those very pointy ears
She'd got a thick coat of fur
She was very fit.

Soda was old
So that was that.

Her whiskers so incredibly long
She always used to lick me in the morning
Soda was old
So that was that.

Alex Smith (10)
Winchester House School, Brackley

Trigger

My dog Trigger was a wonder dog
Now my thoughts are full of him

His bright yellow eyes
Were a big surprise
But when my mum and dad were afar
He ran straight back to the car.

My dog Trigger was a wonder dog
Now my thoughts are full of him

His long pink tongue,
Was a long pink snake,
His fur was as soft,
As a king sized duvet.

My dog Trigger was a wonder dog
Now my thoughts are full of him

But now that he is dead
We have thrown away his bed.

My dog Trigger was a wonder dog
Now my thoughts are full of him.

Ben Seymour
Winchester House School, Brackley

Tarragon

He was big and furry
And smiled a cheesy grin at you.
He let the dogs sit on his back
And even kissed them. Oooh
He never did a tiny little thing wrong.

He's been gone for a bit too long.

He ate my ice creams and everything else
And he nibbled your pockets, waiting for treats.
He was fat and friendly
And as he got older he got greedy.

He's been gone for a bit too long.

He had a squidgy saddle that we have still got.
He has a very soft rug that is for my pony now.
He won loads of things in those days
He was just amazing in many ways.
I had known him my whole life.

He's been gone for a bit too long.

Lucinda Sewell (10)
Winchester House School, Brackley

Albert

Albert's gone:
I can't help that.

Admitted he was dying
With a small squeaky voice;
Always wore the same green jumper,
As green as grass.
The brown shoes always shiny;
Had small ears like his shoes;
Was thin as a 30cm ruler

Albert's gone:
I can't help that.

Had hair as white as snow;
White skin like his hair.
Every winter, at the window,
Looking at the ice skaters.
Sat in the same armchair
Like a snuggled rabbit.

Albert's gone:
I can't help that.

Pierre Scrase (10)
Winchester House School, Brackley

Great Grandpa

My great grandpa died aged ninety;
My mum was sad.

He was in the army;
Captured by the Japanese and survived;
He went to live in Cornwall,
His wife died.
He had a great smart checked jacket;
He had huge great slippers;
He loved to sail
When the weather was fine.

My great grandpa died aged ninety;
I was sad.

He went to live in an old people's home.
He smelt of biscuits
He was a very good chess player;
He taught in a prep school.
He played lots of hockey.
He had a shiny walking stick.
His birthday was on bonfire night.

My great grandpa died aged ninety;
We all miss him.

Ned Rodger (10)
Winchester House School, Brackley

Grandad's Gone

*Grandad's gone now
I am sad.*

He had old clothes and
A big brown hat
A beaky brown nose
Wiry grey hair.

*Grandad's gone and
Now Dad's sad.*

He always said 'Crikey.'
With a kind low voice
Was most certain to have a joke
Fun to mess around with.

*Grandad's gone and
Now we are all sad.*

Alexander Burns (10)
Winchester House School, Brackley

Geordie

Geordie, he was as small as a mouse.
He had blonde hair like a yellow piece of paper.
His eyes are as blue as the sky.

Now he's left I miss him greatly.

Geordie, he was as amusing as a clown
He was as fast as an antelope.
He was as brave as a lion.

Now he's left I miss him greatly.

Geordie, he had a cold swimming pool in his garden.
He played on his Nintendo all the time.
He had about ten horses and eleven fields.

Now he's left I miss him greatly.

Sam Pointon (10)
Winchester House School, Brackley

Lynn Chadwick – My Grandpa

I loved the way he had no sense of humour
And he had big ears, but could not hear well.

*But I loved Lynn
And I won't see him.*

He had to go around in his buggy
And in his three hundred acre valley he drove.

*But I loved Lynn
And I won't see him.*

His big warm hands
Grooved from making sculptures.

*But I loved Lynn
And I won't see him.*

His sculpture's best, Teddy Boy and Girl
That's my grandpa and now he is gone

*And I loved Lynn
But I won't see him.*

Emily Marchant (10)
Winchester House School, Brackley

Joey

*Now Joey's gone
And I miss him.*

Flowing white mane
Stuck up like Beckham's,
Gleaming white coat
Shining like shoe polish,
Small pointing hooves
As Billy Elliot's,
Hair as messy as a haystack,
Joking little face
As a Thelwell's,
Feathered fetlocks
That brushed the ground,
Eyes as quick as light.

*Now Joey's gone
And I miss him.*

He was as funny as a clown
From the biggest circus,
Looked after like a doctor,
Jumped like a kangaroo,
Loved carrots more than anything,
Came to me like a magnet.

*Now Joey's gone
And I miss him.*

Polly Mainds (10)
Winchester House School, Brackley

Alick Rankin

He died before the millennium,
Everyone cried especially my mum.

A head of grey feathers
On a bird's wing;
He liked picnics,
Chocolates,
And long days of shooting.

He died before the millennium,
Everyone cried especially my mum.

He had a pudding bowl for a stomach,
He liked to sit and drink wine,
He adored good food.

He died before the millennium,
Everyone cried especially my mum.

He loved his three dogs,
He liked to watch birds,
He told me how to recognise each one,
He'd take me for rides on his tractor,
And I'd be sad when we were done.

He died before the millennium,
Everyone cried especially my mum.

When I go back to the house these days,
I miss him more than ever,
Then I realise when he'll come back:
Never.

Tom Lynas (10)
Winchester House School, Brackley

Big Pa Pa

*Big Pa Pa's gone
And I'm sad about that.*

His big old face
With a huge smile
I used to stroke his soft grey hair
His big blue eyes always laughed
His big old feet were always gentle
His big hands with fleecy mittens

*Big Pa Pa's gone
And I'm sad about that.*

He wore a big cuddly jumper
He gave me a hedgehog
That I've still got
His soft ancient armchair
He was tall if he stood up
I sent a picture to him
That he never got.

*Big Pa Pa's gone
And I'm sad about that.*

Sophie Lees-Millais (10)
Winchester House School, Brackley

Star

Star had a good life,
And I'm glad about that.

Twinkle star eyes
Gleaming through the day,
Seeing myself in her eyes
And food as she nibbled away.

Star had a good life
And I'm glad about that.

Soft fur had Star,
Orange, black and snow white
In patches everywhere.

Star had a good life,
And I'm glad about that.

Small pointed claws,
That never scratched me,
Stroke her all day, I would,
As she sniffed all around her surroundings.

Star had a good life,
And I'm glad about that.

My favourite was her stride,
Scrabbling around her home,
Climbing on top of her food bowl,
Ascending up the side searching around me,
Searching around me.

Star had a good life
And I'm glad about that.

Philip Hart (9)
Winchester House School, Brackley

My Auntie's Dog Brucey

Brucey has passed away
I'm sorry to say.

He was a Doberman,
He had sleek black fur
Like a silhouette
A rough wet nose
Black as the end of
Tiger's tail.
Lovely brown eyes
I was nine when he died.

Brucey has passed away
I'm sorry to say.

He would run round and round
In circles
And bite his tail
When we left him at my auntie's house
He would wail.
He smelt like leather and grass
He would sleep on the sofa
Would chase anything he saw.

Brucey has passed away
I'm sorry to say.

Michael Evans (10)
Winchester House School, Brackley

My Brother Alex

He is far away and
I can't see him.

He has a big fat face
Like a monkey.
He has short brown hair
Like a slimy slug.

He is far away
And I can't see him.

He shouts like a whale
That's being tortured.
He is as sad as someone
Who has just died.

He is far away
And I can't see him.

His T-shirt is as rough as a
Crumpled up leaf
When you scratch it feels as if
You're scratching a chalk board.
He is far away
And I can't see him.

Siobhan Dick (9)
Winchester House School, Brackley

My Dog Henry

My dog is dead
But had a good life.

He was white with a brown patch
Had a waggly tail
He loved going on long walks
And always gave his toys to me wanting me to
Play with him.

My dog is dead
But had a good life.

He had his own room with a bed with shelves of toys
But he kept running away around the village
And the lady from up the road complained
At least five times

My dog is dead
But had a good life

He loved playing footie with me
He was the best dog of all
We came back from holiday and
Henry, my dog, was dead.

Louis de Watteville (9)
Winchester House School, Brackley

Great Grandpa

*I'm sad to say
That GG's passed away.*

He would tickle with his fluffy moustache,
Touch your nose saying 'Honk honk.'
If he caught you in a game
He would tickle you.
His laughing made you laugh.
Smelt of freshly ironed clothes;
Drank milk from his bowl;
Eyebrows were fluffy and grey
Like a thick forest.

*I'm sad to say
That GG's passed away.*

Hazel coloured quick eyes,
Hair always was flat and grey
With soft white streaks,
He would chase you around the house
Pretending to be a ghost.

*I'm sad to say
That GG's passed away.*

Emma Crawfurd (9)
Winchester House School, Brackley

Maxi

*My dog Maxi was put down
I felt sad and angry.*

I miss:
His short brown fur,
His big fine brown ears,
His madness with bowls,
His small paddy feet,
His long pointed tail.

*My dog Maxi was put down
I felt sad and angry.*

I miss:
His long whiskers as hard as plastic,
His small paw going into the goldfish bowl,
His blue lonely eyes,
He loved to sleep on my bed at night,
He made me laugh,
He was always there for me.

*My dog Maxi was put down
I felt sad and angry.*

Alex Comfort
Winchester House School, Brackley

Grandpa

Grandpa has gone
I wish he'd come back.

Grandpa had a hairy beard
Low loud laugh
He read me stories at night.

Grandpa has gone
I wish he'd come back.

His white fluffy hair
He would sit in his big armchair
His square glasses.

Grandpa has gone
I wish he'd come back

He loved the beach
His eyes were deep blue
Wore old clothes, didn't care
Food would stick in his beard.

Grandpa has gone
I wish he'd come back.

William Clarke (10)
Winchester House School, Brackley

My Old Cat

My cat Ferret
Was good at catching mice,
Liked eating Hula Hoops
He thought they were nice.
He was a striped tabby
Like his sister Firkin.

But when Ferret died,
It was a shame because,
He couldn't eat his hula hoops again.

He liked to sleep on the cooker,
We knew that because,
He purred loudly.
He jumped on top of the cupboard,
And with help from Firkin,
He opened the door.

But when Ferret died
It was a shame,
Because Firkin couldn't
Open the door again.

Rowan Brogden (10)
Winchester House School, Brackley

Uncle Ted

*Uncle Ted's dead and
I'm sorry about that.*

He had a big laugh,
He had shiny teeth,
He went on walks,
He had hair on the side of his head,
He had big hands,
He was funny.

*Uncle Ted's dead and
I'm sorry about that.*

He was always trying to help,
He wore a leather coat,
And a browny yellow hat,
He was always active,
He was always telling jokes,
He gave us lemonade and a biscuit.

*Now he's dead and
I'm sorry about that.*

James Bowden (10)
Winchester House School, Brackley

Ralphy

Ralph used to run away all the time,
If he didn't know you he'd bark,
He was a Cairn terrier, grey and tan,

Now he's dead,
And there's no other dog like him.

He used to chew his basket,
His favourite toy was a little furry dog,
It was ripped and torn,
He had very sharp teeth,
And he loved bouncing balls on his nose.

Now he's dead,
And there's no other dog like him.

When we went on holiday he rescued another dog,
Both his eyes were brown,
He was 7 months when he got run over.

Now he's dead,
And there's no other dog like him.

Florence Cain
Winchester House School, Brackley

Katherine

She has a happy smile,
And a funny laugh.

But now we've moved away,
So I can't see her anymore.

She will always listen,
But she talks a lot.

But now we've moved away,
So I can't see her anymore.

She has two annoying brothers,
And a loving mum.

But now we've moved away,
So I can't see her anymore.

She has a small house,
With big, windy stairs.

But now we've moved away,
So I can't see her anymore.

Harriett Clitheroe (11)
Winchester House School, Brackley

Fireworks

F lames from the fireworks
I ndigo and red
R eaching the air in a screechy voice
E *xplosions* happening all the time
W hen the fireworks are over we all go back to the fire
O range colours warming up the night
R emember, remember the fifth of November
K eep your pets indoors and they'll be fine
S pectacular, spitting, blazing lights because that's Bonfire Night!

Emily Ratcliffe (9)
Woodton CP School, Bungay

The Dragon

D ragging its tail in the red hot lava
R oaring, showing its mighty dragon teeth
A glint of killer instinct in its eye
G ripping the corpse of a dead man in its jaws
O n the floor lies a dead woman!
N obody dares come to the cave.

Kai Garrett (10)
Woodton CP School, Bungay

The Giant

G iants are tall
I n boots, cloaks with clubs
A nd if you go too close
N asty giants might strike
T he horrible man is bad
S cary, frightening and mad!

Ben Walker (9)
Woodton CP School, Bungay

Fairy

F luttering through the ice-white frost
A long a bed of flowers
I n a dress of sparkles and glitter
R ound and round the frosted towers
Y ou'll see her pass by in the cold.

Hannah Tynan (11)
Woodton CP School, Bungay

My Baby Brother

My mum said I could hold the baby for a photograph.
I was very nervous but I took the challenge.
It was very soft and squidgy.

When the photo was taken,
I was relieved to give it back to my mum.

I was so glad that I didn't drop it,
If I did I would have got told off.

My baby brother has got brown tufty hair, with tiny fingers.
His fingernails are tiny too and the same with his toes.
He is three months old.
I can't wait for him to be old enough to play football
With me.

Jamie Ellis (8)
Woodton CP School, Bungay

My Baby Sister

All of us were at the theme park,
We were walking straight along the path.
Mum gave me the baby
And Mum said 'I'm going to take a photo of you
Two together.'

We decided to stand at the toy stall
I froze and began to shake, I thought I was going
To drop her.
But everything was OK
I can't wait to go out again.

Tara Constable (9)
Woodton CP School, Bungay

My Baby Brother

I felt so jealous of that tiny thing more special than me.
I got so mad that I fell over and grazed my knee.

'Don't worry, it's nothing,' Mum said.
I felt like a bomb had hit the house
And I was the only survivor.

Mum said 'Would you like to hold your brother?'
I was terrified of the thing that was more special than me.
'No, no, no,' I shouted!

Rachel McAvilley (7)
Woodton CP School, Bungay

Monday's Child

Monday's child has very black teeth
Tuesday's child is a very good thief
Wednesday's child has a very runny nose
Thursday's child uses a hose
Friday's child breaks the vase
Saturday's child drives lots of cars
But the child that is born on the seventh day,
Won't use the potty, but that's OK!

Emily Todd (10)
Woodton CP School, Bungay

Fire

F ire bursting
I nto the moonlit night
R oaring into the guy
E ating him away.

Gareth Bush (10)
Woodton CP School, Bungay

Photo Trouble

I heard somebody knock at the door.
It was Penny,
She had brought her baby round for us to see.
Mum said she would take a photo of me holding the baby.

I went and sat on the sofa ready to hold it.
Mum gave it a cuddly bear!

Next Mum put the baby in my arms,
All the pressure came upon me.
Mum was all calm and said it would be fine!

Suddenly I found myself holding it,
Mum got the camera, pressed the button,
Just my luck, nothing happened!

So there I was sitting on the sofa again,
Mum took another photo, it worked this time.
She took the baby and I leapt up fast,
Before they gave the baby back to me again!

Lauren Seely (10)
Woodton CP School, Bungay

Rockets

R oaring as they go against the
O pen black sky
C apturing everybody's eyes
K eep your distance or watch out!
E ach rocket reveals its noisy secret
T o the eyes and ears below
S udden then gone.

Bethany Havers (10)
Woodton CP School, Bungay

My Photo Album

This is a photo of my mate
Paddling in the sea.
A wave was coming behind her,
I'm glad it wasn't me.

This is me in the garden eating ice cream,
Wearing my brand new top.
The ice cream melted and fell on the floor
And my mum had to mop it up.

This is my dog
Who's life is a drag.
His favourite toy
Is a dirty old rag.

This is my mum at my school sports day
See the scratch on her face?
Mum got that when she tripped in the parent's race.

This is my dad
In his brand new suit.
Guess what, he found in his pocket?
A slimy old newt.

Zoë Ratcliffe (11)
Woodton CP School, Bungay

Fairy

F eels like a flower
A lways fluttering around
I n petals of flowers
R unning over the fields
Y ou can always find them.

Gemma Clutten (8)
Woodton CP School, Bungay